SOME PROBLEMS OF
PHILOSOPHY

SOME PROBLEMS OF PHILOSOPHY

A BEGINNING OF AN INTRODUCTION TO PHILOSOPHY

BY

WILLIAM JAMES

GREENWOOD PRESS, PUBLISHERS
NEW YORK   1968

Reprinted with the permission of
David McKay Company, Inc.

Printed in the United States of America

'. . . he [*Charles Renouvier*] *was one of the greatest of philosophic characters, and but for the decisive impression made on me in the seventies by his masterly advocacy of pluralism, I might never have got free from the monistic superstition under which I had grown up. The present volume, in short, might never have been written. This is why, feeling endlessly thankful as I do, I dedicate this text-book to the great Renouvier's memory.*' [*165*]

PREFATORY NOTE

For several years before his death Professor William James cherished the purpose of stating his views on certain problems of metaphysics in a book addressed particularly to readers of philosophy. He began the actual writing of this 'introductory text-book for students in metaphysics,' as he once called it, in March, 1909, and to complete it was at last his dearest ambition. But illness, and other demands on his diminished strength, continued to interfere, and what is now published is all that he had succeeded in writing when he died in August, 1910.

Two typewritten copies of his unfinished manuscript were found. They had been corrected separately. A comparison of the independent alterations in the two copies showed few and slight differences of phrase and detail, and indicated no formed intention to make substantial changes; yet the author perhaps expected to make some further alterations in a final revision if he could finish the book, for in a memorandum dated July 26, 1910, in which he directed the publication of the manuscript, he wrote: '*Say it is fragmentary and unrevised.*'

This memorandum continues, '*Call it "A begin-*

PREFATORY NOTE

ning of an introduction to philosophy." Say that I hoped by it to round out my system, which now is too much like an arch built only on one side.'

In compliance with the author's request left in the same memorandum, his pupil and friend, Dr. H. M. Kallen, has compared the two versions of the manuscript and largely prepared the book for the press. The divisions and headings in the manuscript were incomplete, and for helpful suggestions as to these grateful acknowledgments are also due to Professor R. B. Perry.

HENRY JAMES, JR.

CAMBRIDGE, March 25, 1911.

CONTENTS

CHAPTER I

CHAPTER II

CHAPTER III

CHAPTER IV

CONTENTS

CHAPTER V

CHAPTER VI

CHAPTER VII

CHAPTER VIII

CONTENTS

CHAPTER IX

CHAPTER X

CHAPTER XI

CHAPTER XII

CONTENTS

SOME PROBLEMS OF PHILOSOPHY

SOME PROBLEMS O
PHILOSOPHY

CHAPTER I

PHILOSOPHY AND ITS CRITICS

THE progress of society is due to the fact that individuals vary from the human average in all sorts of directions, and that the originality is often so attractive or useful that they are recognized by their tribe as leaders, and become objects of envy or admiration, and setters of new ideals.

Among the variations, every generation of men produces some individuals exceptionally

Philosophy and those who write it

preoccupied with theory. Such men find matter for puzzle and astonishment where no one else does. Their imagination invents explanations and combines them. They store up the learning of their time, utter prophecies and warnings, and are regarded as sages. Philosophy, etymologically meaning the love of wisdom, is the work of this class of minds, regarded with an indulgent relish, if not with admiration, even by those who do not understand them or believe much in the truth which they proclaim.

3

Philosophy, thus become a race-heritage, forms in its totality a monstrously unwieldy mass of learning. So taken, there is no reason why any special science like chemistry, or astronomy, should be excluded from it. By common consent, however, special sciences are to-day excluded, for reasons presently to be explained; and what remains is manageable **What philosophy is** enough to be taught under the name of philosophy by one man if his interests be broad enough.

If this were a German textbook I should first give my abstract definition of the topic, thus limited by usage, then proceed to display its '*Begriff, und Eintheilung*,' and its '*Aufgabe und Methode.*' But as such displays are usually unintelligible to beginners, and unnecessary after reading the book, it will conduce to brevity to omit that chapter altogether, useful though it might possibly be to more advanced readers as a summary of what is to follow.

I will tarry a moment, however, over the matter of definition. Limited by the omission of the special sciences, the name of philosophy

4

has come more and more to denote ideas of universal scope exclusively. The principles of explanation that underlie all things without exception, the elements common to gods and men and animals and stones, the first *whence* and the last *whither* of the whole cosmic procession, the conditions of all knowing, and the most general rules of human action — these furnish the problems commonly deemed philosophic *par excellence;* and the philosopher is the man who finds the most to say about them. Philosophy is defined in the usual scholastic textbooks as 'the knowledge of things in general by their ultimate causes, so far as natural reason can attain to such knowledge.' This means that explanation of the universe at large, not description of its details, is what philosophy must aim at; and so it happens that a view of anything is termed philosophic just in proportion as it is broad and connected with other views, and as it uses principles not proximate, or intermediate, but ultimate and all-embracing, to justify itself. Any very sweeping view of the world is a philosophy in this sense, even though it may be a vague one. It is a *Weltanschauung*, an intellectualized attitude towards life. Professor Dewey well describes the constitution of all the philosophies that actually exist, when he says that philosophy expresses a certain attitude, purpose and temper of conjoined intellect and will, rather than a discipline whose boundaries can be neatly marked off.[1]

To know the chief rival attitudes towards life, as the history of human thinking has de-Its value veloped them, and to have heard some of the reasons they can give for themselves, ought to be considered an essential part of liberal education. Philosophy, indeed, in one sense of the term is only a compendious name for the spirit in education which the word 'college' stands for in America. Things can be taught in dry dogmatic ways or in a philosophic way. At a technical school a man may grow into a first-rate instrument for doing a certain job, but he may miss all

[1] Compare the article ' Philosophy ' in Baldwin's *Dictionary of Philosophy and Psychology.*

the graciousness of mind suggested by the term liberal culture. He may remain a cad, and not a gentleman, intellectually pinned down to his one narrow subject, literal, unable to suppose anything different from what he has seen, without imagination, atmosphere, or mental perspective.

Philosophy, beginning in wonder, as Plato and Aristotle said, is able to fancy everything different from what it is. It sees the familiar as if it were strange, and the strange as if it were familiar. It can take things up and lay them down again. Its mind is full of air that plays round every subject. It rouses us from our native dogmatic slumber and breaks up our caked prejudices. Historically it has always been a sort of fecundation of four different human interests, science, poetry, religion, and logic, by one another. It has sought by hard reasoning for results emotionally valuable. To have some contact with it, to catch its influence, is thus good for both literary and scientific students. By its poetry it appeals to literary minds; but its logic stiffens them up and remedies their softness. By its logic it appeals to the scientific; but softens them by its other aspects, and saves them from too dry a technicality. Both types of student ought to get from philosophy a livelier spirit, more air, more mental background. 'Hast any philosophy in thee, Shepherd?' — this question of Touchstone's is the one with which men should always meet one another. A man with no philosophy in him is the most inauspicious and unprofitable of all possible social mates.

I say nothing in all this of what may be called the gymnastic use of philosophic study, the purely intellectual power gained by defining the high and abstract concepts of the philosopher, and discriminating between them.

In spite of the advantages thus enumerated, the study of philosophy has systematic *Its enemies and their objections* enemies, and they were never as numerous as at the present day. The definite conquests of science and the apparent indefiniteness of philosophy's results partly account for this; to say nothing of man's native rudeness of mind, which maliciously

enjoys deriding long words and abstractions.
'Scholastic jargon,' 'mediæval dialectics,' are
for many people synonyms of the word philosophy. With his obscure and uncertain speculations as to the intimate nature and causes
of things, the philosopher is likened to a
'blind man in a dark room looking for a black
hat that is not there.' His occupation is described as the art of 'endlessly disputing
without coming to any conclusion,' or more
contemptuously still as the *systematische Miss-
brauch einer eben zu diesem Zwecke erfundenen
Terminologie.*'

Only to a very limited degree is this sort of
hostility reasonable. I will take up some of the
current objections in successive order, since to
reply to them will be a convenient way of
entering into the interior of our subject.

Objection 1. Whereas the sciences make
steady progress and yield applications of matchless utility, philosophy
makes no progress and has no practical applications.

Objec-
tion that
it is un-
practical
answered

Reply. The opposition is unjustly founded,

for the sciences are themselves branches of the tree of philosophy. As fast as questions got accurately answered, the answers were called 'scientific,' and what men call 'philosophy' to-day is but the residuum of questions still unanswered. At this very moment we are seeing two sciences, psychology and general biology, drop off from the parent trunk and take independent root as specialties. The more general philosophy cannot as a rule follow the voluminous details of any special science.

A backward glance at the evolution of philosophy will reward us here. The earliest philosophers in every land were encyclopædic sages, lovers of wisdom, sometimes with, and sometimes without a dominantly ethical or religious interest. They were just men curious beyond immediate practical needs, and no particular problems, but rather the problematic generally, was their specialty. China, Persia, Egypt, India, had such wise men, but those of Greece are the only sages who until very recently have influenced the course of western thinking. The

This objection in the light of history

10

earlier Greek philosophy lasted, roughly speaking, for about two hundred and fifty years, say from 600 B. C. onwards. Such men as Thales, Heracleitus, Pythagoras, Parmenides, Anaxagoras, Empedocles, Democritus, were mathematicians, theologians, politicians, astronomers, and physicists. All the learning of their time, such as it was, was at their disposal. Plato and Aristotle continued their tradition, and the great mediæval philosophers only enlarged its field of application. If we turn to Saint Thomas Aquinas's great 'Summa,' written in the thirteenth century, we find opinions expressed about literally everything, from God down to matter, with angels, men, and demons taken in on the way. The relations of almost everything with everything else, of the creator with his creatures, of the knower with the known, of substances with forms, of mind with body, of sin with salvation, come successively up for treatment. A theology, a psychology, a system of duties and morals, are given in fullest detail, while physics and logic are established in their universal principles.

The impression made on the reader is of almost superhuman intellectual resources. It is true that Saint Thomas's method of handling the mass of fact, or supposed fact, which he treated, was different from that to which we are accustomed. He deduced and proved everything, either from fixed principles of reason, or from holy Scripture. The properties and changes of bodies, for example, were explained by the two principles of matter and form, as Aristotle had taught. Matter was the quantitative, determinable, passive element; form, the qualitative, unifying, determining, and active principle. All activity was for an end. Things could act on each other only when in contact. The number of species of things was determinate, and their differences discrete, etc., etc.[1]

By the beginning of the seventeenth century, men were tired of the elaborate *a priori* methods of scholasticism. Suarez's treatises availed not

[1] J. Rickaby's *General Metaphysics* (Longmans, Green and Co.) gives a popular account of the essentials of St. Thomas's philosophy of nature. Thomas J. Harper's *Metaphysics of the School* (Macmillan) goes into minute detail.

to keep them in fashion. But the new philosophy of Descartes, which displaced the
scholastic teaching, sweeping over Europe like
wildfire, preserved the same encyclopædic
character. We think of Descartes nowadays
as the metaphysician who said 'Cogito, ergo
sum,' separated mind from matter as two contrasted substances, and gave a renovated proof
of God's existence. But his contemporaries
thought of him much more as we think of
Herbert Spencer in our day, as a great cosmic
evolutionist, who explained, by 'the redistribution of matter and motion,' and the laws of
impact, the rotations of the heavens, the circulation of the blood, the refraction of light, apparatus of vision and of nervous action, the
passions of the soul, and the connection of the
mind and body.

Descartes died in 1650. With Locke's
'Essay Concerning Human Understanding,'
published in 1690, philosophy for the first time
turned more exclusively to the problem of
knowledge, and became 'critical.' This subjective tendency developed; and although the

school of Leibnitz, who was the pattern of a universal sage, still kept up the more universal tradition — Leibnitz's follower Wolff published systematic treatises on everything, physical as well as moral — Hume, who succeeded Locke, woke Kant 'from his dogmatic slumber,' and since Kant's time the word 'philosophy' has come to stand for mental and moral speculations far more than for physical theories. Until a comparatively recent time, philosophy was taught in our colleges under the name of 'mental and moral philosophy,' or 'philosophy of the human mind,' exclusively, to distinguish it from 'natural philosophy.'

But the older tradition is the better as well as the completer one. To know the actual peculiarities of the world we are born into is surely as important as to know what makes worlds anyhow abstractly possible. Yet this latter knowledge has been treated by many since Kant's time as the only knowledge worthy of being called philosophical. Common men feel the question 'What is Nature like?' to be as meritorious as the Kantian question 'How is Nature possible?' So philosophy, in order not to lose human respect, must take some notice of the actual constitution of reality. There are signs to-day of a return to the more objective tradition.[1]

Philosophy in the full sense is only *man thinking*, thinking about generalities rather than about particulars. But whether about generalities or particulars, man thinks always by the same methods. He observes, discriminates, generalizes, classifies, looks for causes, traces analogies, and makes hypotheses. Philosophy, taken as something distinct from science or from practical affairs, follows no method peculiar to itself. All our thinking to-day has evolved gradually out of primitive human thought, and the only really important changes that have come over its manner (as distinguished from the matters in which it believes) are a greater hesitancy in asserting its convic-

Philosophy is only 'man thinking'

[1] For an excellent defence of it I refer my readers to Paulsen's *Introduction to Philosophy*, translated by Thilly (1895), pp. 19–44.

tions, and the habit of seeking verification[1] for them whenever it can.

It will be instructive to trace very briefly the origins of our present habits of thought.

Auguste Comte, the founder of a philosophy which he called 'positive,'[2] said that human

Origin of man's present ways of thinking

theory on any subject always took three forms in succession. In the theological stage of theorizing, phe-nomena are explained by spirits pro-ducing them; in the metaphysical stage, their essential feature is made into an abstract idea, and this is placed behind them as if it were an explanation; in the positive stage, phenomena are simply described as to their coexistences and successions. Their 'laws' are formulated, but no explanation of their natures or existence is sought after. Thus a *'spiritus rector'* would be a theological,—a 'principle of attraction' a metaphysical,—and a 'law of the squares' would be a positive theory of the planetary movements.

[1] Compare G. H. Lewes: *Aristotle* (1864), chap. 4.
[2] *Cours de philosophie positive*, 6 volumes, Paris, 1830–1842.

16

Comte's account is too sharp and definite. Anthropology shows that the earliest attempts at human theorizing mixed the theological and metaphysical together. Common things needed no special explanation, remarkable things alone, odd things, especially deaths, calamities, diseases, called for it. What made things act was the mysterious energy in them, and the more awful they were, the more of this *mana* they possessed. The great thing was to acquire *mana* oneself. 'Sympathetic magic' is the collective name for what seems to have been the primitive philosophy here. You could act on anything by controlling anything else that either was associated with it or resembled it. If you wished to injure an enemy, you should either make an image of him, or get some of his hair or other belongings, or get his name written. Injuring the substitute, you thus made him suffer correspondingly. If you wished the rain to come, you sprinkled the ground, if the wind, you whistled, etc. If you would have yams grow well in your garden, put a stone there that looks like a yam. Would you cure jaundice, give tumeric, that makes things look yellow; or give poppies for troubles of the head, because their seed vessels form a 'head.' This 'doctrine of signatures' played a great part in early medicine. The various '-mancies' and '-mantics' come in here, in which witchcraft and incipient science are indistinguishably mixed. 'Sympathetic' theorizing persists to the present day. 'Thoughts are things,' for a contemporary school — and on the whole a good school — of practical philosophy. Cultivate the thought of what you desire, affirm it, and it will bring all similar thoughts from elsewhere to reinforce it, so that finally your wish will be fulfilled.[1]

Little by little, more positive ways of considering things began to prevail. Common elements in phenomena began to be singled out and to form the basis of generalizations. But these elements at first had necessarily to be the

[1] Compare Prentice Mulford and others of the ' new thought' type. For primitive sympathetic magic consult J. Jastrow in *Fact and Fable in Psychology*, the chapter on Analogy; F. B. Jevons: *Introduction to the History of Religion*, chap. iv; J. G. Frazer: *The Golden Bough*, i, 2; R. R. Marett : *The Threshold of Religion*, *passim* ; A. O. Lovejoy : *The Monist*, xvi, 357.

more dramatic or humanly interesting ones. The hot, the cold, the wet, the dry in things explained their behavior. Some bodies were naturally warm, others cold. Motions were natural or violent. The heavens moved in circles because circular motion was the most perfect. The lever was explained by the greater quantity of perfection embodied in the movement of its longer arm.[1] The sun went south in winter to escape the cold. Precious or beautiful things had exceptional properties. Peacock's flesh resisted putrefaction. The lodestone would drop the iron which it held if the superiorly powerful diamond was brought near, etc.

Such ideas sound to us grotesque, but imagine no tracks made for us by scientific ancestors, and what aspects would we single out from nature to understand things by? Not till the beginning of the seventeenth century did the more insipid kinds of regularity in things abstract men's attention away from the prop-

[1] On Greek science, see W. Whewell's *History of the Inductive Sciences*, vol. i, book i; G. H. Lewes, *Aristotle*, *passim*.

erties originally picked out. Few of us realize how short the career of what we know as 'science' has been. Three hundred and fifty years ago hardly any one believed in the Copernican planetary theory. Optical combinations were not discovered. The circulation of the blood, the weight of air, the conduction of heat, the laws of motion were unknown; the common pump was inexplicable; there were no clocks; no thermometers; no general gravitation; the world was five thousand years old; spirits moved the planets; alchemy, magic, astrology, imposed on every one's belief. Modern science began only after 1600, with Kepler, Galileo, Descartes, Torricelli, Pascal, Harvey, Newton, Huygens, and Boyle. Five men telling one another in succession the discoveries which their lives had witnessed, could deliver the whole of it into our hands: Harvey might have told Newton, who might have told Voltaire; Voltaire might have told Dalton, who might have told Huxley, who might have told the readers of this book.

The men who began this work of emancipa-

tion were philosophers in the original sense of
the word, universal sages. Galileo said that

Science is
special-
ized phi-
losophy he had spent more years on philosophy than months on mathematics.
Descartes was a universal philosopher in the fullest sense of the term. But the
fertility of the newer conceptions made special
departments of truth grow at such a rate that
they became too unwieldy with details for the
more universal minds to carry them, so the
special sciences of mechanics, astronomy, and
physics began to drop off from the parent stem.

No one could have foreseen in advance the
extraordinary fertility of the more insipid
mathematical aspects which these geniuses fer-
reted out. No one could have dreamed of the
control over nature which the search for their
concomitant variations would give. 'Laws' describe these variations; and all our present laws
of nature have as their model the proportionality of v to t, and of s to t^2 which Galileo first
laid bare. Pascal's discovery of the proportionality of altitude to barometric height, Newton's of acceleration to distance, Boyle's of

air-volume to pressure, Descartes' of sine to cosine in the refracted ray, were the first fruits of Galileo's discovery. There was no question of agencies, nothing animistic or sympathetic in this new way of taking nature. It was description only, of concomitant variations, after the particular quantities that varied had been successfully abstracted out. The result soon showed itself in a differentiation of human knowledge into two spheres, one called 'Science,' within which the more definite laws apply, the other ' General Philosophy,' in which they do not. The state of mind called positivistic is the result. 'Down with philosophy!' is the cry of innumerable scientific minds. 'Give us measurable facts only, phenomena, without the mind's additions, without entities or principles that pretend to explain.' It is largely from this kind of mind that the objection that philosophy has made no progress, proceeds.

It is obvious enough that if every step forward which philosophy makes, every question to which an accurate answer is found, gets ac-

credited to science the residuum of unanswered problems will alone remain to constitute the domain of philosophy, and will alone bear her name. In point of fact this is just what is happening. Philosophy has become a collective name for questions that have not

Philosophy is the residuum of problems unsolved by science

yet been answered to the satisfaction of all by whom they have been asked. It does not follow, because some of these questions have waited two thousand years for an answer, that no answer will ever be forthcoming. Two thousand years probably measure but one paragraph in that great romance of adventure called the history of the intellect of man. The extraordinary progress of the last three hundred years is due to a rather sudden finding of the way in which a certain order of questions ought to be attacked, questions admitting of mathematical treatment. But to assume therefore, that the only possible philosophy must be mechanical and mathematical, and to disparage all enquiry into the other sorts of question, is to forget the extreme diversity of aspects under which reality undoubtedly exists. To the spiritual questions the proper avenues of philosophic approach will also undoubtedly be found. They have, to some extent, been found already. In some respects, indeed, 'science' has made less progress than 'philosophy' — its most general conceptions would astonish neither Aristotle nor Descartes, could they revisit our earth. The composition of things from elements, their evolution, the conservation of energy, the idea of a universal determinism, would seem to them commonplace enough — the little things, the microscopes, electric lights, telephones, and details of the sciences, would be to them the awe-inspiring things. But if they opened our books on metaphysics, or visited a philosophic lecture room, everything would sound strange. The whole idealistic or 'critical' attitude of our time would be novel, and it would be long before they took it in.[1]

Objection 2. Philosophy is dogmatic, and

---

[1] The reader will find all that I have said, and much more, set forth in an excellent article by James Ward in *Mind,* vol. 15, no. lviii: 'The Progress of Philosophy.'

pretends to settle things by pure reason, whereas the only fruitful mode of getting at truth is to appeal to concrete experience. Science collects, classes, and analyzes facts, and thereby far outstrips philosophy.

Reply. This objection is historically valid. Too many philosophers have aimed at closed systems, established *a priori*, claiming infallibility, and to be accepted or rejected only as totals. The sciences on the other hand, using hypotheses only, but always seeking to verify them by experiment and observation, open a way for indefinite self-correction and increase. At the present day, it is getting more and more difficult for dogmatists claiming finality for their systems, to get a hearing in educated circles. Hypothesis and verification, the watchwords of science, have set the fashion too strongly in academic minds.

Philosophy need not be dogmatic

Since philosophers are only men thinking about things in the most comprehensive possible way, they can use any method whatsoever freely. Philosophy must, in any case, complete the sciences, and must incorporate their methods. One cannot see why, if such a policy should appear advisable, philosophy might not end by forswearing all dogmatism whatever, and become as hypothetical in her manners as the most empirical science of them all.

Objection 3. Philosophy is out of touch with real life, for which it substitutes abstractions. The real world is various, tangled, painful. Philosophers have, almost without exception, treated it as noble, simple, and perfect, ignoring the complexity of fact, and indulging in a sort of optimism that exposes their systems to the contempt of common men, and to the satire of such writers as Voltaire and Schopenhauer. The great popular success of Schopenhauer is due to the fact that, first among philosophers, he spoke the concrete truth about the ills of life.

Reply. This objection also is historically valid, but no reason appears why philosophy

Nor is it divorced from reality should keep aloof from reality permanently. Her manners may change as she successfully develops. The thin and noble abstractions may give way to more solid and real constructions, when the materials and methods for making such constructions shall be more and more securely ascertained. In the end philosophers may get into as close contact as realistic novelists with the facts of life.

In conclusion. In its original acceptation, meaning the completest knowledge of the universe, philosophy must include the results of all the sciences, and cannot be contrasted with the latter. It simply aims at making of science what Herbert Spencer calls a 'system of completely unified knowledge.'[1] In the more modern sense, of something contrasted with the sciences, philosophy means 'metaphysics.' The older sense is the more worthy sense, and as the results of the sciences get more available for co-ordination, and the conditions for finding truth in different kinds of question get more methodically defined, we may hope that the term will revert to its original meaning. Science, meta-

Philosophy as metaphysics

---

[1] See the excellent chapter in Spencer's *First Principles*, entitled: ' Philosophy Defined.'

SOME PROBLEMS OF PHILOSOPHY

physics, and religion may then again form a
single body of wisdom, and lend each other
mutual support.

At present this hope is far from its fulfil-
ment. I propose in this book to take philosophy in the narrow sense of metaphysics, and
to let both religion and the results of the sciences alone.

CHAPTER II

THE PROBLEMS OF METAPHYSICS

No exact definition of the term 'metaphysics' is possible, and to name some of the prob-
Examples of metaphysical problems lems it treats of is the best way of getting at the meaning of the word. It means the discussion of various obscure, abstract, and universal questions which the sciences and life in general suggest but do not solve; questions left over, as it were; questions, all of them very broad and deep, and relating to the whole of things, or to the ultimate elements thereof. Instead of a definition let me cite a few examples, in a random order, of such questions: —

What are 'thoughts,' and what are 'things'? and how are they connected?

What do we mean when we say 'truth'?

Is there a common stuff out of which all facts are made?

How comes there to be a world at all? and, Might it as well not have been?

Which is the most real kind of reality?

What binds all things into one universe?

Is unity or diversity more fundamental?

Have all things one origin? or many?

Is everything predestined, or are some things (our wills for example) free?

Is the world infinite or finite in amount?

Are its parts continuous, or are there vacua?

What is God? — or the gods?

How are mind and body joined? Do they act on each other?

How does anything act on anything else?

How can one thing change or grow out of another thing?

Are space and time beings? — or what?

In knowledge, how does the object get into the mind? — or the mind get at the object?

We know by means of universal notions. Are these also real? Or are only particular things real?

What is meant by a 'thing'?

'Principles of reason,' — are they inborn or derived?

Are 'beauty' and 'good' matters of opinion

only? Or have they objective validity? And, if so, what does the phrase mean?

Such are specimens of the kind of question termed metaphysical. Kant said that the three essential metaphysical questions were: —

What can I know?

What should I do?

What may I hope?

A glance at all such questions suffices to rule out such a definition of metaphysics as that of **Meta-physics defined** Christian Wolff, who called it 'the science of what is possible,' as distinguished from that of what is actual, for most of the questions relate to what is actual fact. One may say that metaphysics inquires into the cause, the substance, the meaning, and the outcome of all things. Or one may call it the science of the most universal principles of reality (whether experienced by us or not), in their connection with one another and with our powers of knowledge. 'Principles' here may mean either entities, like 'atoms,' 'souls,' or logical laws like: 'A thing must either exist or not exist'; or generalized facts, like 'things can act only

after they exist.' But the principles are so numerous, and the 'science' of them is so far from
completion, that such definitions have only a
decorative value. The serious work of metaphysics is done over the separate single questions. If these should get cleared up, talk of metaphysics as a unified science might properly begin. This book proposes to handle only a few
separate problems, leaving others untouched.

These problems are for the most part real;
that is, but few of them result from a misuse
Nature of   of terms in stating them. 'Things,'
meta-
physical   for example, are or are not composed
problems   of one stuff; they either have or have
not a single origin; they either are or are not
completely predetermined, etc. Such alternatives may indeed be impossible of decision;
but until this is conclusively proved of them,
they confront us legitimately, and some one
must take charge of them and keep account of
the solutions that are proposed, even if he does
not himself add new ones. The opinions of the
learned regarding them must, in short, be
classified and responsibly discussed. For in-

stance, how many opinions are possible as to the origin of the world? Spencer says that the world must have been either eternal, or self-created, or created by an outside power. So for him there are only three. Is this correct? If so, which of the three views seems the most reasonable? and why? In a moment we are in the thick of metaphysics. We have to be meta-physicians even to decide with Spencer that neither mode of origin is thinkable and that the whole problem is unreal.

Some hypotheses may be absurd on their face, because they are self-contradictory. If, for example, infinity means 'what can never be completed by successive syntheses,' the notion of anything made by the successive addition of infinitely numerous parts, and yet completed, is absurd. Other hypotheses, for example that everything in nature contributes to a single supreme purpose, may be insuscep-tible either of proof or of disproof. Other hypotheses again, for instance that vacua exist, may be susceptible of probable solution. The classing of the hypotheses is thus as necessary as the classing of the problems, and both must be recognized as constituting a serious branch of learning.[1] There must in short be metaphysicians. Let us for a while become metaphysicians ourselves.

As we survey the history of metaphysics we soon realize that two pretty distinct types of

Rational-ism and empiri-cism in meta-physics

mind have filled it with their war-fare. Let us call them the rationalist and the empiricist types of mind. A saying of Coleridge's is often quoted, to the effect that every one is born either a platonist or an aristotelian. By aristotelian, he means empiricist, and by platonist, he means rationalist; but although the contrast between the two Greek philosphers exists in the sense in which Coleridge meant it, both of them were rationalists as compared with the kind of empiricism which Democritus and Protagoras developed; and Coleridge had better have taken either of those names instead of Aris-totle as his empiricist example.

[1] Consult here Paul Janet: *Principes de Métaphysique*, etc., 1897, leçons 1, 2.

Rationalists are the men of principles, empiricists the men of facts; but, since principles are universals, and facts are particulars, perhaps the best way of characterizing the two tendencies is to say that rationalist thinking proceeds most willingly by going from wholes to parts, while empiricist thinking proceeds by going from parts to wholes. Plato, the arch-rationalist, explained the details of nature by their participation in 'ideas,' which all depended on the supreme idea of the 'good.' Protagoras and Democritus were empiricists. The latter explained the whole cosmos, including gods as well as men, and thoughts as well as things, by their composition out of atomic elements; Protagoras explained truth, which for Plato was the absolute system of the ideas, as a collective name for men's opinions.

Rationalists prefer to deduce facts from principles. Empiricists prefer to explain principles as inductions from facts. Is thought for the sake of life? or is life for the sake of thought? Empiricism inclines to the former, rationalism to the latter branch of the alternative. God's life, according to Aristotle and Hegel, is pure theory. The mood of admiration is natural to rationalism. Its theories are usually optimistic, supplementing the experienced world by clean and pure ideal constructions. Aristotle and Plato, the Scholastics, Descartes, Spinoza, Leibnitz, Kant, and Hegel are examples of this. They claimed absolute finality for their systems, in the noble architecture of which, as their authors believed, truth was eternally embalmed. This temper of finality is foreign to empiricist minds. They may be dogmatic about their method of building on 'hard facts,' but they are willing to be sceptical about any conclusions reached by the method at a given time. They aim at accuracy of detail rather than at completeness; are contented to be fragmentary; are less inspiring than the rationalists, often treating the high as a case of 'nothing but' the low ('nothing but' self-interest well understood, etc.), but they usually keep more in touch with actual life, are less subjective, and their spirit is obviously more 'scientific' in the hackneyed sense of that term. Socrates, Locke, Berkeley, Hume, the Mills, F. A. Lange, J. Dewey, F. C. S. Schiller, Bergson, and other contemporaries are specimens of this type. Of course we find mixed minds in abundance, and few philosophers are typical in either class. Kant may fairly be called mixed. Lotze and Royce are mixed. The author of this volume is weakly endowed on the rationalist side, and his book will show a strong leaning towards empiricism. The clash of the two ways of looking at things will be emphasized throughout the volume.[1]

I will now enter the interior of the subject by discussing special problems as examples of metaphysical inquiry; and in order not to conceal any of the skeletons in the philosophic closet, I will start with the worst problem possible, the so-called 'ontological problem,' or question of how there comes to be anything at all.

[1] Compare W. James: 'The Sentiment of Rationality,' in *The Will to Believe* (Longmans, Green and Co., 1899), p. 63 f.; *Pragmatism*, (ibid.), chap. i; *A Pluralistic Universe* (ibid.), chap. i.

CHAPTER III

THE PROBLEM OF BEING

How comes the world to be here at all instead of the nonentity which might be imagined in its place? Schopenhauer's remarks on this question may be considered classical. 'Apart from man,' he says, 'no being wonders at its own existence. When man first becomes conscious, he takes himself for granted, as something needing no explanation. But not for long; for, with the rise of the first reflection,

Schopenhauer on the origin of the problem that wonder begins which is the mother of metaphysics, and which made Aristotle say that men now and always seek to philosophize because of wonder — The lower a man stands in intellectual respects the less of a riddle does existence seem to him . . . but, the clearer his consciousness becomes the more the problem grasps him in its greatness. In fact the unrest which keeps the never stopping clock of metaphysics going is the thought that the non-existence of this world is just as possible as its existence. Nay more, we soon conceive the world as something the non-existence of which not only is conceivable but would indeed be preferable to its existence; so that our wonder passes easily into a brooding over that fatality which nevertheless could call such a world into being, and mislead the immense force that could produce and preserve it into an activity so hostile to its own interests. The philosophic wonder thus becomes a sad astonishment, and like the overture to Don Giovanni, philosophy begins with a minor chord.' [1]

One need only shut oneself in a closet and begin to think of the fact of one's being there, of one's queer bodily shape in the darkness (a thing to make children scream at, as Stevenson says), of one's fantastic character and all, to have the wonder steal over the detail as much as over the general fact of being, and to see that it is only familiarity that blunts it. Not only that *anything* should be, but that *this* very thing should be, is mysterious! Philoso-

[1] *The World as Will and Representation:* Appendix 17, 'On the metaphysical need of man,' abridged.

phy stares, but brings no reasoned solution,
for from nothing to being there is no logical
bridge.

Attempts are sometimes made to banish the
question rather than to give it an answer.
Those who ask it, we are told, extend illegit-
imately to the whole of being the contrast
Various to a supposed alternative non-being
treatments
of the which only particular beings possess.
problem These, indeed, were not, and now
are. But being in general, or in some shape,
always was, and you cannot rightly bring the
whole of it into relation with a primordial nonentity. Whether as God or as material atoms,
it is itself primal and eternal. But if you call
any being whatever eternal, some philosophers
have always been ready to taunt you with the
paradox inherent in the assumption. Is past
eternity completed? they ask: If so, they go on,
it must have had a beginning; for whether
your imagination traverses it forwards or backwards, it offers an identical content or stuff to
be measured; and if the amount comes to an
end in one way, it ought to come to an end in

the other. In other words, since we now witness its end, some past moment must have witnessed its beginning. If, however, it had a beginning, when was that, and why?

You are up against the previous nothing, and do not see how it ever passed into being. This dilemma, of having to choose between a regress which, although called infinite, has nevertheless come to a termination, and an absolute first, has played a great part in philosophy's history.

Other attempts still are made at exorcising the question. Non-being is not, said Parmenides and Zeno; only being is. Hence what is, is necessarily being — being, in short, is necessary. Others, calling the idea of nonentity no real idea, have said that on the absence of an idea can no genuine problem be founded. More curtly still, the whole ontological wonder has been called diseased, a case of *Grübelsucht* like asking, 'Why am I myself?' or 'Why is a triangle a triangle?'

Rationalistic minds here and there have sought to reduce the mystery. Some forms of being have been deemed more natural, so to say, or more inevitable and necessary than others. Empiricists of the evolution-

Rational-
ist and
empiricist
treatments ary type — Herbert Spencer seems a good example — have assumed that whatever had the least of reality, was weakest, faintest, most imperceptible, most nascent, might come easiest first, and be the earliest successor to nonentity. Little by little the fuller grades of being might have added themselves in the same gradual way until the whole universe grew up.

To others not the minimum, but the maximum of being has seemed the earliest First for the intellect to accept. 'The perfection of a thing does not keep it from existing,' Spinoza said, 'on the contrary, it founds its existence.' [1] It is mere prejudice to assume that it is harder for the great than for the little to be, and that easiest of all it is to be nothing. What makes things difficult in any line is the alien obstructions that are met with, and the smaller and weaker the thing the more powerful over it

[1] *Ethics*, part i, prop. xi, scholium.

these become. Some things are so great and inclusive that to be is implied in their very nature. The anselmian or ontological proof of God's existence, sometimes called the cartesian proof, criticised by Saint Thomas, rejected by Kant, re-defended by Hegel, follows this line of thought. What is conceived as imperfect may lack being among its other lacks, but if God, who is expressly defined as *Ens perfectissimum*, lacked anything whatever, he would contradict his own definition. He cannot lack being therefore: He is *Ens necessarium, Ens realissimum*, as well as *Ens perfectissimum*.[1]

Hegel in his lordly way says: 'It would be strange if God were not rich enough to embrace so poor a category as Being, the poorest and most abstract of all.' This is somewhat in line with Kant's saying that a real dollar does not contain one cent more than an imaginary dollar. At the beginning of his logic Hegel seeks in another way to mediate nonentity with being.

[1] St. Anselm: *Proslogium*, etc. Translated by Doane: Chicago, 1903; Descartes: *Meditations*, p. 5; Kant: *Critique of Pure Reason, Transcendental Dialectic*, 'On the impossibility of an ontological proof, etc.'

Since 'being' in the abstract, mere being, means nothing in particular, it is indistinguishable from 'nothing'; and he seems dimly to think that this constitutes an identity between the two notions, of which some use may be made in getting from one to the other. Other still queerer attempts show well the rationalist temper. Mathematically you can deduce 1 from 0 by the following process: $\frac{0}{0}=\frac{1-1}{1-1}=1$. Or physically if all being has (as it seems to have) a 'polar' construction, so that every positive part of it has its negative, we get the simple equation: $+1-1=0$, *plus* and *minus* being the signs of polarity in physics.

It is not probable that the reader will be satisfied with any of these solutions, and contemporary philosophers, even rationalistically minded ones, have on the whole agreed that no one has intelligibly banished the mystery of *fact*. Whether the original nothing burst into God and vanished, as night vanishes in day, while God thereupon became the creative principle of all lesser beings; or whether all things have foisted or shaped themselves imperceptibly into existence, the same amount of existence has in the end to be assumed

The same amount of existence must be begged by all and begged by the philosopher. To comminute the difficulty is not to quench it. If you are a rationalist you beg a kilogram of being at once, we will say; if you are an empiricist you beg a thousand successive grams; but you beg the same amount in each case, and you are the same beggar whatever you may pretend. You leave the logical riddle untouched, of how the coming of whatever is, came it all at once, or came it piecemeal, can be intellectually understood.[1]

If being gradually *grew*, its quantity was of course not always the same, and may not be

Conservation vs. creation the same hereafter. To most philosophers this view has seemed absurd, neither God, nor primordial matter, nor energy being supposed to admit of increase or decrease. The orthodox opinion is that the

---

[1] In more technical language, one may say that fact or being is 'contingent,' or matter of 'chance,' so far as our intellect is concerned. The conditions of its appearance are uncertain, unforeseeable, when future, and when past, elusive.

quantity of reality must at all costs be con-
served, and the waxing and waning of our
phenomenal experiences must be treated as
surface appearances which leave the deeps untouched.

Nevertheless, within experience, phenomena
come and go. There are novelties; there are
losses. The world seems, on the concrete and
proximate level at least, really to grow. So the
question recurs: How do our finite experiences
come into being from moment to moment?
By inertia? By perpetual creation? Do the
new ones come at the call of the old ones? Why
do not they all go out like a candle?

Who can tell off-hand? The question of being is the darkest in all philosophy. All of us
are beggars here, and no school can speak dis-
dainfully of another or give itself superior airs.
For all of us alike, Fact forms a datum, gift, or
Vorgefundenes, which we cannot burrow under,
explain or get behind. It makes itself somehow, and our business is far more with its
What than with its Whence or Why.

CHAPTER IV

PERCEPT AND CONCEPT—THE IMPORT OF CONCEPTS

THE problem convenient to take up next in order will be that of the difference between thoughts and things. 'Things' are known to us by our senses, and are called 'presentations' by some authors, to distinguish them from the ideas or 'representations' which we may have when our senses are closed. I myself have grown accustomed to the words 'percept' and 'concept' in treating of the contrast, but concepts flow out of percepts and into them again,

Their difference they are so interlaced, and our life rests on them so interchangeably and undiscriminatingly, that it is often difficult to impart quickly to beginners a clear notion of the difference meant. Sensation and thought in man are mingled, but they vary independently. In our quadrupedal relatives thought proper is at a minimum, but we have no reason to suppose that their immediate life of feeling is either less or more copious than ours. Feel-

47

ing must have been originally self-sufficing; and thought appears as a superadded function, adapting us to a wider environment than that of which brutes take account. Some parts of the stream of feeling must be more intense, emphatic, and exciting than others in animals as well as in ourselves; but whereas lower animals simply react upon these more salient sensations by appropriate movements, higher animals remember them, and men react on them intellectually, by using nouns, adjectives, and verbs to identify them when they meet them elsewhere.

The great difference between percepts and concepts[1] is that percepts are continuous and concepts are discrete. Not discrete in their *being*, for conception as an *act* is part of the flux of feeling, but discrete from each other in their several *meanings*. Each concept means

---

[1] In what follows I shall freely use synonyms for these two terms. 'Idea,' 'thought,' and 'intellection' are synonymous with 'concept.' Instead of 'percept' I shall often speak of 'sensation,' 'feeling,' 'intuition,' and sometimes of 'sensible experience' or of the 'immediate flow' of conscious life. Since Hegel's time what is simply perceived has been called the 'immediate,' while the 'mediated' is synonymous with what is conceived.

just what it singly means, and nothing else; and if the conceiver does not know whether he means this or means that, it shows that his concept is imperfectly formed. The perceptual flux as such, on the contrary, *means* nothing, and is but what it immediately is. No matter how small a tract of it be taken, it is always a much-at-once, and contains innumerable aspects and characters which conception can pick out, isolate, and thereafter always intend. It shows duration, intensity, complexity or simplicity, interestingness, excitingness, pleasantness or their opposites. Data from all our senses enter into it, merged in a general extensiveness of which each occupies a big or little share. Yet all these parts leave its unity unbroken. Its boundaries are no more distinct than are those of the field of vision. Boundaries are things that intervene; but here nothing intervenes save parts of the perceptual flux itself, and these are overflowed by what they separate, so that whatever we distinguish and isolate conceptually is found perceptually to telescope and compenetrate and diffuse into its neighbors. The cuts we make are purely ideal. If my reader can succeed in abstracting from all conceptual interpretation and lapse back into his immediate sensible life at this very moment, he will find it to be what some-one has called a big blooming buzzing confusion, as free from contradiction in its 'much-at-onceness' as it is all alive and evidently there.[1]

Out of this aboriginal sensible muchness attention carves out objects, which conception then names and identifies forever—

The conceptual order

in the sky 'constellations,' on the earth 'beach,' 'sea,' 'cliff,' 'bushes,' 'grass.' Out of time we cut 'days' and 'nights,' 'summers' and 'winters.' We say *what* each part of the sensible continuum is, and all these abstracted *whats* are concepts.[2]

[1] Compare W. James: *A Pluralistic Universe*, pp. 282-288. Also *Psychology, Briefer Course*, pp. 157-166.

[2] On the function of conception consult: Sir William Hamilton's *Lectures on Logic*, 9, 10; H. L. Mansel, *Prolegomena Logica*, chap. i; A. Schopenhauer, *The World as Will*, etc., Supplements 6, 7 to book ii; W. James, *Principles of Psychology*, chap. xii; *Briefer Course*, chap. xiv. Also J. G. Romanes: *Mental Evolution in Man*, chaps. iii, iv; Th. Ribot: *l'Evolution des Idées Générales*, chap. vi; Th. Ruyssen, *Essai sur l'Evolution psychologique du Jugement*, chap. vii; Laromiguière, *Leçons de Phil-*

PERCEPT AND CONCEPT

The intellectual life of man consists almost wholly in his substitution of a conceptual order for the perceptual order in which his experience originally comes. But before tracing the consequences of the substitution, I must say something about the conceptual order itself.[1]

Trains of concepts unmixed with percepts grow frequent in the adult mind; and parts of these conceptual trains arrest our attention just as parts of the perceptual flow did, giving rise to concepts of a higher order of abstractness. So subtile is the discernment of man, and so great the power of some men to single out

osophie, part 2, lesson 12. The account I give directly contradicts that which Kant gave which has prevailed since Kant's time. Kant always speaks of the aboriginal sensible flux as a 'manifold' of which he considers the essential character to be its disconnectedness. To get any togetherness at all into it requires, he thinks, the agency of the 'transcendental ego of apperception,' and to get any definite connections requires the agency of the understanding, with its synthetizing concepts or 'categories.' 'Die Verbindung (conjunctio) eines Mannigfaltigen kann überhaupt niemals durch Sinne in uns kommen, und kann also auch nicht in der reinen Form der sinnlichen Anschauung zugleich mit enthalten sein; denn sie ist ein Actus der Spontaneität der Einbildungskraft, und, da man diese, zum Unterschiede von der Sinnlichkeit, Verstand nennen muss, so ist alle Verbindung . . . eine Verstandeshandlung.' K. d. r. V., 2te, Aufg., pp. 129–130. The reader must decide which account agrees best with his own actual experience.

[1] The substitution was first described in these terms by S. H. Hodgson in his *Philosophy of Reflection*, i, 288–310.

the most fugitive elements of what passes before them, that these new formations have no limit. Aspect within aspect, quality after quality, relation upon relation, absences and negations as well as present features, end by being noted and their names added to the store of nouns, verbs, adjectives, conjunctions, and prepositions by which the human mind interprets life. Every new book verbalizes some new concept, which becomes important in proportion to the use that can be made of it. Different universes of thought thus arise, with specific sorts of relation among their ingredients. The world of common-sense 'things'; the world of material tasks to be done; the mathematical world of pure forms; the world of ethical propositions; the worlds of logic, of music, etc., all abstracted and generalized from long forgotten perceptual instances, from which they have as it were flowered out, return and merge themselves again in the particulars of our present and future perception. By those *whats* we apperceive all our *thises*. Percepts and concepts interpenetrate and melt together, impregnate and fertilize each other. Neither, taken alone, knows reality in its completeness. We need them both, as we need both our legs to walk with.

From Aristotle downwards philosophers have frankly admitted the indispensability, for complete knowledge of fact, of both the sensational and the intellectual contribution.[1] For complete knowledge of fact, I say; but facts are particulars and connect themselves with practical necessities and the arts; and Greek philosophers soon formed the notion that a knowledge of so-called 'universals,' consisting of concepts of abstract forms, qualities, numbers, and relations was the only knowledge worthy of the truly philosophic mind. Particular facts decay and our perceptions of them vary. A concept never varies; and between such unvarying terms the relations must be constant and express eternal verities. Hence there arose a tendency, which has lasted all through philosophy, to contrast the know-

[1] See, for example, book i, chap. ii, of Aristotle's *Metaphysics*.

SOME PROBLEMS OF PHILOSOPHY

ledge of universals and intelligibles, as god-
like, dignified, and honorable to the knower,
with that of particulars and sensibles as something relatively base which more allies us with
the beasts.[1]

[1] Plato in numerous places, but chiefly in books 6 and 7 of the *Re-
public*, contrasts perceptual knowledge as 'opinion' with real knowledge, to the latter's glory. For an excellent historic sketch of this
platonistic view see the first part of E. Laas's *Idealismus und Positivis-
mus*, 1879. For expressions of the ultra-intellectualistic view, read the
passage from *Plotinus on the Intellect* in C. M. Bakewell's *Source-book
in Ancient Philosophy*, N. Y. 1907, pp. 353 f.; Bossuet, *Traité de la
Connaissance de Dieu*, chap. iv, §§ v, vi; R. Cudworth, *A Treatise concerning eternal amd immutable Morality*, books iii, iv. — 'Plato,' writes
Prof. Santayana, 'thought that all the truth and meaning of earthly
things was the reference they contained to a heavenly original. This
heavenly original we remember to recognize even among the distor-
tions, disappearances, and multiplications of its ephemeral copies. . . .
The impressions themselves have no permanence, no intelligible essence, but are always either arising or ceasing to be. There must be,
he tells us, an eternal and clearly definable object of which the visible
appearances to us are the multiform semblance; now by one trait,
now by another, the phantom before us reminds us of that half-
forgotten celestial reality and makes us utter its name. . . . We and
the whole universe exist only in the attempt to return to our perfection, to lose ourselves again in God. That ineffable good is our natural possession; and all we honor in this life is but a partial recovery
of our birthright; every delightful thing is like a rift in the clouds,
through which we catch a glimpse of our native heaven. And if that
heaven seems so far away, and the idea of it so dim and unreal, it is
because we are so far from perfect, so immersed in what is alien and
destructive to the soul.' ('Platonic Love in some Italian Poets,' in
Interpretations of Poetry and Religion, 1896.)

This is the interpretation of Plato which has been current since

PERCEPT AND CONCEPT

For rationalistic writers conceptual knowledge was not only the more noble knowledge, but it originated independently of all perceptual particulars. Such concepts as God, perfection, eternity, infinity, immutability, identity, absolute beauty, truth, justice, necessity, freedom, duty, worth, etc., and the part they play in our mind, are, it was supposed, impossible to explain as results of practical experience. The empiricist view, and probably the true view, is that they do result from practical experience.[1] But a more important question than that as to the origin of our concepts is that as to their

Conceptual knowledge — the rationalist view

Aristotle. It should be said that its profundity has been challenged by Prof. A. J. Stewart. (Plato's *Doctrine of Ideas*, Oxford, 1909.)

Aristotle found great fault with Plato's treatment of ideas as heavenly originals, but he agreed with him fully as to the superior excellence of the conceptual or theoretic life. In chapters vii and viii of book x of the *Nicomachean Ethics* he extols contemplation of universal relations as alone yielding pure happiness. ' The life of God, in all its exceeding blessedness, will consist in the exercise of philosophic thought; and of all human activities, that will be the happiest which is most akin to the divine.'

[1] John Locke, in his *Essay concerning Human Understanding*, books i, ii, was the great popularizer of this doctrine. Condillac's *Traité des Sensations*, Helvetius's work, *De l'Homme*, and James Mill's *Analysis of the Human Mind*, were more radical successors of Locke's great book.

functional use and value; — is *that* tied down to perceptual experience, or out of all relation to it? Is conceptual knowledge self-sufficing and a revelation all by itself, quite apart from its uses in helping to a better understanding of the world of sense?

Rationalists say, Yes. For, as we shall see in later places (page 68), the various conceptual universes referred to on page 52 can be considered in complete abstraction from perceptual reality, and when they are so considered, all sorts of fixed relations can be discovered among their parts. From these the *a priori* sciences of logic, mathematics, ethics, and æsthetics (so far as the last two can be called sciences at all) result. Conceptual knowledge must thus be called a self-sufficing revelation; and by rationalistic writers it has always been treated as admitting us to a diviner world, the world of universal rather than that of perishing facts, of essential qualities, immutable relations, eternal principles of truth and right. Emerson writes: 'Generalization is always a new influx of divinity into the mind: hence the thrill that attends it.' And a disciple of Hegel, after exalting the knowledge of 'the General, Unchangeable, and alone Valuable' above that of 'the Particular, Sensible and Transient,' adds that if you reproach philosophy with being unable to make a single grass-blade grow, or even to know how it does grow, the reply is that since such a particular 'how' stands not above but below knowledge, strictly so-called, such an ignorance argues no defect.[1]

To this ultra-rationalistic opinion the empiricist contention that *the significance of concepts consists always in their relation to perceptual particulars* has been opposed. Made of percepts, or distilled from parts of percepts, their essential office, it has been said, is to coalesce with percepts again, bringing the mind back into the perceptual world with a better command of the situation there. Certainly whenever we *can* do this with our concepts, we do *more* with

Concept-
ual know-
ledge —
the em-
piricist
view

---

[1] Michelet, Hegel's *Werke*, vii, 15, quoted by A. Gratry, *De la Connaissance de l'Âme*, i, 231. Compare the similar claim for philosophy in W. Wallace's *Prolegomena to Hegel*, 2d ed., 1894, pp. 28–29, and the long and radical statement of the same view in book iv of Ralph Cudworth's *Treatise on Eternal and Immutable Morality*.

them than when we leave them flocking with their abstract and motionless companions. It is possible therefore, to join the rationalists in allowing conceptual knowledge to be self-sufficing, while at the same time one joins the empiricists in maintaining that the full *value* of such knowledge is got only by combining it with perceptual reality again. This mediating attitude is that which this book must adopt. But to understand the nature of concepts better we must now go on to distinguish their *function* from their *content*.

The concept 'man,' to take an example, is three things: 1, the word itself; 2, a vague picture of the human form which has its own value in the way of beauty or not; and 3, an instrument for symbolizing certain objects from which we may expect human treatment when occasion arrives. Similarly of 'triangle,' 'cosine,'— they have their substantive value both as words and as images suggested, but they also have a functional value whenever they lead us elsewhere in discourse.

The content and function of concepts

There are concepts, however, the image-part of which is so faint that their whole value seems to be functional. 'God,' 'cause,' 'number,' 'substance,' 'soul,' for example, suggest no definite picture; and their significance seems to consist entirely in their *tendency*, in the further turn which they may give to our action or our thought.[1] We cannot rest in the contemplation of their form, as we can in that of a 'circle' or a 'man'; we must pass beyond.

Now however beautiful or otherwise worthy of stationary contemplation the substantive part of a concept may be, the more important part of its significance may naturally be held to be the consequences to which it leads. These may lie either in the way of making us think, or in the way of making us act. Whoever has a clear idea of these knows effectively what the concept practically signifies, whether its substantive content be interesting in its own right or not.

The prag-
matic rule

This consideration has led to a method of

---

[1] On this functional tendency compare H. Taine, *On Intelligence*, book i, chap. ii (1870).

interpreting concepts to which I shall give the name of *the Pragmatic Rule*.[1]

The pragmatic rule is that the meaning of a concept may always be found, if not in some sensible particular which it directly designates, then in some particular difference in the course of human experience which its being true will make. Test every concept by the question 'What sensible difference to anybody will its truth make?' and you are in the best possible position for understanding what it means and for discussing its importance. If, questioning whether a certain concept be true or false, you can think of absolutely nothing that would practically differ in the two cases, you may assume that the alternative is meaningless and that your concept is no distinct idea. If two concepts lead you to infer the same particular consequence, then you may assume that they embody the same meaning under different names.

This rule applies to concepts of every order

---

[1] Compare W. James, *Pragmatism*, chap. ii and *passim;* also Baldwin's *Dictionary of Philosophy*, article ' Pragmatism,' by C. S. Peirce.

of complexity, from simple terms to propositions uniting many terms.

So many disputes in philosophy hinge upon ill-defined words and ideas, each side claiming its own word or idea to be true, that any accepted method of making meanings clear must be of great utility. No method can be handier of application than our pragmatic rule. If you claim that any idea is true, assign at the same time some difference that its being true will make in some possible person's history, and we shall know not only just what you are really claiming but also how important an issue it is, and how to go to work to verify the claim. In obeying this rule we neglect the substantive content of the concept, and follow its function only. This neglect might seem at first sight to need excuse, for the content often has a value of its own which might conceivably add lustre to reality, if it existed, apart from any modification wrought by it in the other parts of reality. Thus it is often supposed that 'Idealism' is a theory precious in itself, even though no definite change in the details of our experience can be deduced from it. Later discussion will show that this is a superficial view, and that particular consequences are the only criterion of a concept's meaning, and the only test of its truth.

Instances are hardly called for, they are so obvious. That A and B are 'equal,' for example, **Examples** means either that 'you will find no difference' when you pass from one to the other, or that in substituting one for the other in certain operations 'you will get the same result both times.' 'Substance' means that 'a definite group of sensations will recur.' 'Incommensurable' means that 'you are always confronted with a remainder.' 'Infinite' means either that, or that 'you can count as many units in a part as you can in the whole.' 'More' and 'less' mean certain sensations, varying according to the matter. 'Freedom' means 'no feeling of sensible restraint.' 'Necessity' means that 'your way is blocked in all directions save one.' 'God' means that 'you can dismiss certain kinds of fear,' 'cause' that 'you may expect certain sequences,' etc. etc.

We shall find plenty of examples in the rest of
this book; so I go back now to the more general
question of whether the whole import of the
world of concepts lies in its relation to perceptual experience, or whether it be also an independent revelation of reality. Great ambiguity
is possible in answering this question, so we
must mind our Ps and Qs.

The first thing to notice is that in the earliest
stages of human intelligence, so far as we can
guess at them, thought proper must have had
an exclusively practical use. Men classed their
Origin of   sensations, substituting concepts for
concepts   them, in order to 'work them for
in their
utility   what they were worth,' and to pre-
pare for what might lie ahead. Class-names
suggest consequences that have attached
themselves on other occasions to other members of the class — consequences which the
present percept will also probably or certainly
show.[1] The present percept in its immediacy
may thus often sink to the status of a bare sign

[1] For practical uses of conception compare W. James, *Principles of
Psychology*, chap. xxii; J. E. Miller, *The Psychology of Thinking*, 1909,
passim, but especially chaps. xv, xvi, xvii.

of the consequences which the substituted concept suggests.

The substitution of concepts and their
connections, of a whole conceptual order, in
short, for the immediate perceptual flow, thus
widens enormously our mental panorama. Had
we no concepts we should live simply 'getting'
each successive moment of experience, as the
sessile sea-anemone on its rock receives whatever nourishment the wash of the waves may
bring. With concepts we go in quest of the absent, meet the remote, actively turn this way or
that, bend our experience, and make it tell us
whither it is bound. We change its order, run
it backwards, bring far bits together and separate near bits, jump about over its surface instead of plowing through its continuity, string
its items on as many ideal diagrams as our
mind can frame. All these are ways of *handling*
the perceptual flux and *meeting* distant parts of
it; and as far as this primary function of conception goes, we can only conclude it to be
what I began by calling it, a faculty superadded
to our barely perceptual consciousness for its

use in practically adapting us to a larger environment than that of which brutes take account.[1] We *harness* perceptual reality in concepts in order to drive it better to our ends.

Does our conceptual translation of the perceptual flux enable us also to understand the latter better? What do we mean by making us 'understand'? Applying our pragmatic rule to the interpretation of the word, we see that the better we understand anything the more we are able to *tell about it*. Judged by this test, concepts do make us understand our percepts better: knowing *what* these are, we can tell all sorts of farther truths about them, based on the relation of those whats to other whats. The whole system of relations, spatial, temporal, and logical, of our fact, gets plotted out. An ancient philosophical opinion, inherited from Aristotle, is that we do not understand a thing until we know it by its causes. When the maidservant says that 'the cat' broke the tea-cup,

The theo-
retic use
of con-
cepts

[1] Herbert Spencer in his *Psychology*, parts iii and iv, has at great length tried to show that such adaptation is the sole meaning of our intellect.

she would have us conceive the fracture in a causally explanatory way. No otherwise when Clerk-Maxwell asks us to conceive of gas-electricity as due to molecular bombardment. An imaginary agent out of sight becomes in each case a part of the cosmic context in which we now place the percept to be explained; and the explanation is valid in so far as the new causal *that* is itself conceived in a context that makes its existence probable, and with a nature agreeable to the effects it is imagined to produce. All our scientific explanations would seem to conform to this simple type of the 'necessary cat.' The conceived order of nature built round the perceived order and explaining it theoretically, as we say, is only a system of hypothetically imagined *thats*, the *whats* of which harmoniously connect themselves with the *what* of any *that* which we immediately perceive.

The system is essentially a topographic system, a system of the distribution of things. It tells us what's what, and where's where. In so far forth it merely prolongs that opening up of the perspective of practical consequences which we found to be the primordial utility of the conceiving faculty: it adapts us to an immense environment. Working by the causes of things we gain advantages which we never should have compassed had we worked by the things alone.

But in order to reach such results the concepts in the explanatory system must, I said, In the *a* 'harmoniously connect.' What does *priori* sciences that mean? Is this also only a practical advantage, or is it something more? It seems something more, for it points to the fact that when concepts of various sorts are once abstracted or constructed, new relations are then found between them, connecting them in peculiarly intimate, 'rational,' and unchangeable ways. In another book[1] I have tried to show that these rational relations are all products of our faculty of comparison and of our sense of 'more.'

The sciences which exhibit these relations are the so-called *a priori* sciences of mathe-

---

[1] *Principles of Psychology*, 1890, chap. xxviii.

matics and logic.[1] But these sciences express relations of comparison and identification exclusively. Geometry and algebra, for example, first define certain conceptual objects, and then establish equations between them, substituting equals for equals. Logic has been defined as the 'substitution of similars'; and in general one may say that the perception of likeness and unlikeness generates the whole of 'rational' or 'necessary' truth. Nothing *happens* in the worlds of logic, mathematics or moral and æsthetic preference. The static nature of the relations in these worlds is what gives to the propositions that express them their 'eternal' character: The binomial theorem, e. g., expresses the value of any power of any sum of two terms, to the end of time.

These vast unmoving systems of universal terms form the new worlds of thought of which I spoke on page 56. The terms are elements (or are framed of elements) abstracted from

[1] The 'necessary' character of the abstract truths which these sciences exhibit is well explained by G. H. Lewes: *Problems of Life and Mind*, Problem 1, chapters iv, xiii, especially p. 405 f. of the English edition (1874).

the perceptual flux; but in their abstract shape we note relations between them (and again between these relations) which enable us to set up various schemes of fixed serial orders or of 'more and more.' The terms are indeed man-made, but the order, being established solely by comparison, is fixed by the nature of the terms on the one hand and by our power of perceiving relations on the other. Thus two abstract twos are always the same as an abstract four; what contains the container contains the contained of whatever material either be made; equals added to equals always give equal results, in the world in which abstract equality is the only property the terms are supposed to possess; the more than the more is more than the less, no matter in what direction of moreness we advance; if you dot off a term in one series every time you dot one off in another, the two series will either never end, or will come to an end together, or one will be exhausted first, etc. etc.; the result being those skeletons of 'rational' or 'necessary' truth in which our logic- and mathematics-books (sometimes our philosophy-books) arrange their universal terms.

The 'rationalization' of any mass of perceptual fact consists in assimilating its concrete terms, one by one, to so many terms of the conceptual series, and then in assuming that the relations intuitively found among the latter are what connect the former too. Thus we rationalize gas-pressure by identifying it with the blows of hypothetic molecules; then we see that the more closely the molecules are crowded the more frequent the blows upon the containing walls will become; then we discern the exact proportionality of the crowding with the number of blows; so that finally Mariotte's empirical law gets rationally explained. All our transformations of the sense-order into a more rational equivalent are similar to this one. We interrogate the beautiful apparition, as Emerson calls it, which our senses ceaselessly raise upon our path, and the items there refer us to their interpretants in the shape of ideal constructions in some static arrangement which our

And in physics

mind has already made out of its concepts
alone. The interpretants are then substituted
for the sensations, which thus get rationally
conceived. To 'explain' means to coördinate,
one to one, the *thises* of the perceptual flow
with the *whats* of the ideal manifold, whichever
it be.[1]

We may well call this a theoretic conquest
over the order in which nature originally comes.
The conceptual order into which we translate
our experience seems not only a means of practical adaptation, but the revelation of a deeper
level of reality in things. Being more constant,
it is *truer*, less illusory than the perceptual
order, and ought to command our attention
more.

There is still another reason why conception
appears such an exalted function. Concepts
Concepts not only guide us over the map of
bring new
values life, but we *revalue* life by their use.
Their relation to percepts is like that of sight
to touch. Sight indeed helps us by preparing

[1] Compare W. Ostwald: *Vorlesungen über Naturphilosophie, Sechste Vorlesung.*

us for contacts while they are yet far off, but it endows us in addition with a new world of optical splendor, interesting enough all by itself to occupy a busy life. Just so do concepts bring their proper splendor. The mere possession of such vast and simple pictures is an inspiring good: they arouse new feelings of sublimity, power, and admiration, new interests and motivations.

Ideality often clings to things only when they are taken thus abstractly. "Causes, as anti-slavery, democracy, etc., dwindle when realized in their sordid particulars. Abstractions will touch us when we are callous to the concrete instances in which they lie embodied. Loyal in our measure to particular ideals, we soon set up abstract loyalty as something of a superior order, to be infinitely loyal to; and truth at large becomes a 'momentous issue' compared with which truths in detail are 'poor scraps, mere crumbling successes.'"[1]

[1] J. Royce: *The Philosophy of Loyalty*, 1908, particularly Lecture vii, § 5.

Emerson writes: 'Each man sees over his own experience a certain stain of error, whilst that of other men looks fair and ideal. Let any

PERCEPT AND CONCEPT

So strongly do objects that come as universal
and eternal arouse our sensibilities, so greatly
do life's values deepen when we translate percepts into ideas! The translation appears as
far more than the original's equivalent.

Concepts thus play three distinct parts in hu-
Summary man life.

1. They steer us practically every day, and
provide an immense map of relations among
the elements of things, which, though not now,
yet on some possible future occasion, may help
to steer us practically;

2. They bring new values into our perceptual
life, they reanimate our wills, and make our
action turn upon new points of emphasis;

3. The map which the mind frames out of

man go back to those delicious relations which make the beauty of his
life, which have given him sincerest instruction and nourishment, he
will shrink and moan. Alas! I know not why, but infinite compunc-
tions embitter in mature life the remembrances of budding joy, and
cover every beloved name. Everything is beautiful seen from the point
of view of the intellect, or as truth, but all is sour, if seen as experience.
Details are melancholy; the plan is seemly and noble. In the actual
world — the painful kingdom of time and place — dwell care, and
canker, and fear. With thought, with the ideal, is immortal hilarity,
the rose of Joy. Round it all the muses sing. But grief clings to names
and persons, and the partial interests of to-day and yesterday.' (*Essay
on Love.*)

them is an object which possesses, when once it has been framed, an independent existence. It suffices all by itself for purposes of study. The 'eternal' truths it contains would have to be acknowledged even were the world of sense annihilated.

We thus see clearly what is gained and what is lost when percepts are translated into concepts. Perception is solely of the here and now; conception is of the like and unlike, of the future, of the past, and of the far away. But this map of what surrounds the present, like all maps, is only a surface; its features are but abstract signs and symbols of things that in themselves are concrete bits of sensible experience. We have but to weigh extent against content, thickness against spread, and we see that for some purposes the one, for other purposes the other, has the higher value. Who can decide offhand which is absolutely better to live or to understand life? We must do both alternately, and a man can no more limit himself to either than a pair of scissors can cut with a single one of its blades.

CHAPTER V

PERCEPT AND CONCEPT — THE ABUSE OF CONCEPTS [1]

In spite of this obvious need of holding our percepts fast if our conceptual powers are to mean anything distinct, there has always been a tendency among philosophers to treat conception as the more essential thing in know-

The in-
tellectual-
ist creed

ledge. [2] The Platonizing persuasion has ever been that the intelligible order ought to supersede the senses rather than interpret them. The senses, according to this opinion, are organs of wavering illusion that stand in the way of 'knowledge,' in the unalterable sense of that term. They are an unfortunate complication on which philosophers may safely turn their backs.

'Your sensational modalities,' writes one of

[1] [This chapter and the following chapter do not appear as separate chapters in the manuscript. Ed.]

[2] The traditional rationalist view would have it that to understand life, without entering its turmoil, is the absolutely better part. Philosophy's 'special work,' writes William Wallace, 'is to comprehend the world, not try to make it better' (*Prolegomena to the Study of Hegel's Philosophy*, 2d edition, Oxford, 1894, p. 29).

these, 'are but darkness, remember that.
Mount higher, up to reason, and you will see
light. Impose silence on your senses, your
imagination, and your passions, and you will
then hear the pure voice of interior truth, the
clear and evident replies of our common mis-
tress [reason]. Never confound that evidence
which results from the comparison of ideas
with the vivacity of those feelings which move
and touch you. . . . We must follow reason
despite the caresses, the threats and the in-
sults of the body to which we are conjoined,
despite the action of the objects that surround
us. . . . I exhort you to recognize the difference there is between knowing and feeling,
between our clear ideas, and our sensations
always obscure and confused.'[1]

This is the traditional intellectualist creed.
When Plato, its originator, first thought of
concepts as forming an entirely separate world
and treated this as the only object fit for the
study of immortal minds, he lit up an entirely

[1] Malebranche: *Entretiens sur la Métaphysique*, 3me. Entretien,
viii, 9.

new sort of enthusiasm in the human breast. These objects were precious objects, concrete things were dross. Introduced by Dion, who had studied at Athens, to the corrupt and worldly court of the tyrant of Syracuse, Plato, as Plutarch tells us, 'was received with wonderful kindness and respect. . . . The citizens began to entertain marvellous hopes of a speedy reformation when they observed the modesty which now ruled the banquets, and the general decorum which reigned in all the court, their tyrant also behaving himself with gentleness and humanity. . . . There was a general passion for reasoning and philosophy, so much so that the very palace, it is reported, was filled with dust by the concourse of the students in mathematics who were working their problems there ' in the sand. Some ' professed to be indignant that the Athenians, who formerly had come to Syracuse with a great fleet and numerous army, and perished miserably without being able to take the city, should now, by means of one sophister, overturn the sovereignty of Dionysius; inveigling him to cashier his guard of 10,000 lances, dismiss a navy of 400 galleys, disband an army of 10,000 horse and many times over that number of foot, and go seek in the schools an unknown and imaginary bliss, and learn by the mathematics how to be happy.'

Having now set forth the merits of the conceptual translation, I must proceed to show

Defects of the conceptual translation

its shortcomings. We extend our view when we insert our percepts into our conceptual map. We learn *about* them, and of some of them we transfigure the value; but the map remains superficial through the abstractness, and false through the discreteness of its elements; and the whole operation, so far from making things appear more rational, becomes the source of quite gratuitous unintelligibilities. Conceptual knowledge is forever inadequate to the fulness of the reality to be known. Reality consists of existential particulars as well as of essences and universals and class-names, and of existential particulars we become aware only in the perceptual flux. The flux can never be superseded. We must carry it with us to the bitter end of our cognitive business, keeping it in the midst of the translation even when the latter proves illuminating, and falling back on it alone when the translation gives out. 'The insuperability of sensation' would be a short expression of my thesis.

The insuperability of sensation

To prove it, I must show: 1. That concepts are secondary formations, inadequate, and only ministerial; and 2. That they falsify as well as omit, and make the flux impossible to understand.

1. Conception is a secondary process, not indispensable to life. It presupposes perception, which is self-sufficing, as all lower creatures, in whom conscious life goes on by reflex adaptations, show.

To understand a concept you must know what it *means*. It means always some *this*, or some abstract portion of a *this*, with which we first made acquaintance in the perceptual world, or else some grouping of such abstract portions. All conceptual content is borrowed:

to know what the concept 'color' means you must have *seen* red or blue, or green. To know what 'resistance' means, you must have made some effort; to know what 'motion' means, you must have had some experience, active or passive, thereof. This applies as much to concepts of the most rarified order as to qualities like 'bright' and 'loud.' To know what the word 'illation' means one must once have sweated through some particular argument. To know what a 'proportion' means one must have compared ratios in some sensible case. You can create new concepts out of old elements, but the elements must have been perceptually given; and the famous world of universals would disappear like a soap-bubble if the definite contents of feeling, the *thises* and *thats*, which its terms severally denote, could be at once withdrawn. Whether our concepts live by returning to the perceptual world or not, they live by having come from it. It is the nourishing ground from which their sap is drawn.

2. Conceptual treatment of perceptual real-

ity makes it seem paradoxical and incomprehensible; and when radically and consistently carried out, it leads to the opinion that perceptual experience is not reality at all, but an appearance or illusion.

Briefly, this is a consequence of two facts: First, that when we substitute concepts for percepts, we substitute their relations also. But since the relations of concepts are of static comparison only, it is impossible to substitute them for the dynamic relations with which the perceptual flux is filled. Secondly, the conceptual scheme, consisting as it does of discontinuous terms, can only cover the perceptual flux in spots and incompletely. The one is no full measure of the other, essential features of the flux escaping whenever we put concepts in its place.

Why concepts are inadequate

This needs considerable explanation, for we have concepts not only of qualities and relations, but of happenings and actions; and it might seem as if these could make the conceptual order active.[1] But this would be a false

---

[1] Prof. Hibben, in an article in the *Philosophic Review*, vol. xix, pp.

interpretation. The concepts themselves are
fixed, even though they designate parts that
move in the flux; they do not act, even though
they designate activities; and when we substitute them and their order, we substitute a
scheme the intrinsically stationary nature of
which is not altered by the fact that some of
its terms symbolize changing originals. The
concept of 'change,' for example, is always that

125 ff. (1910), seeks to defend the conceptual order against attacks
similar to those in the text, which, he thinks, come from misapprehen-
sions of the true function of logic. ' The peculiar function of thought
is to represent the continuous,' he says, and he proves it by the example of the calculus. I reply that the calculus, in substituting for certain perceptual continuities its peculiar symbols, lets us follow changes
point by point, and is thus their *practical*, but not their *sensible* equivalent. It cannot *reveal* any change to one who never felt it, but it can
lead him to where the change would lead him. It may practically replace the change, but it cannot *reproduce* it. What I am contending
for is that the non-reproducible part of reality is an essential part of
the content of philosophy, whilst Hibben and the logicists seem to
believe that conception, if only adequately attained to, might be all-
sufficient. 'It is the peculiar duty and privilege of philosophy,' Mr.
Hibben writes, ' to exalt the prerogatives of intellect.' He claims that
universals are able to deal adequately with particulars, and that concepts do not so exclude each other, as my text has accused them of
doing. Of course 'synthetic' concepts abound, with subconcepts in-
cluded in them, and the *a priori* world is full of them. But they are
all designative; and I think that no careful reader of my text will accuse me of identifying ' knowledge' with either perception or conception absolutely or exclusively. Perception gives ' intension,' conception gives 'extension ' to our knowledge.

fixed concept. If it changed, its original self would have to stay to mark what it had changed from; and even then the change would be a perceived continuous process, of which the translation into concepts could only consist in the judgment that later and earlier parts of it *differed* — such 'differences' being conceived as absolutely static relations.

Whenever we conceive a thing we *define* it; and if we still don't understand, we define our definition. Thus I define a certain percept by saying 'this is motion,' or 'I am moving'; and then I define motion by calling it the 'being in new positions at new moments of time.' This habit of telling what everything is becomes inveterate. The farther we push it, the more we learn *about* our subject of discourse, and we end by thinking that knowing the latter always consists in getting farther and farther away from the perceptual type of experience. This uncriticized habit, added to the intrinsic charm of the conceptual form, is the source of 'intellectualism' in philosophy.

Origin of intellectualism

But intellectualism quickly breaks down. When we try to exhaust motion by conceiving it as a summation of parts, *ad infinitum*, we find only insufficiency.

Inadequacy of intellectualism

Although, when you have a continuum given, you can make cuts and dots in it, *ad libitum*, enumerating the dots and cuts will not give you your continuum back. The rationalist mind admits this; but instead of seeing that the fault is with the concepts, it blames the perceptual flux. This, Kant contends, has no reality in itself, being a mere apparitional birth-place for concepts, to be substituted indefinitely. When these themselves are seen never to attain to a completed sum, reality is sought by such thinkers outside both of the perceptual flow and of the conceptual scheme. Kant lodges it before the flow, in the shape of so-called 'things in themselves';[1] others place it beyond perception, as an Absolute (Bradley), or represent it as a Mind whose

[1] ' We must suppose Noumena,' says Kant, ' in order to set bounds to the objective validity of sense-knowledge' (*Krit. d. reinen Vernunft*, 2d ed., p. 310). The old moral need of somehow rebuking 'Sinnlichkeit'!

ways of thinking transcend ours (Green, the Cairds, Royce). In either case, both our percepts and our concepts are held by such philosophers to falsify reality; but the concepts less than the percepts, for they are static, and by all rationalist authors the ultimate reality is supposed to be static also, while perceptual life fairly boils over with activity and change.

If we take a few examples, we can see how many of the troubles of philosophy come from assuming that to be understood (or 'known' in the only worthy sense of the word) our flowing life must be cut into discrete bits and pinned upon a fixed relational scheme.

Examples of puzzles introduced by conceptual translation

Example 1. *Activity and causation are incomprehensible*, for the conceptual scheme yields nothing like them. Nothing happens therein: concepts are 'timeless,' and can only be juxtaposed and compared. The concept 'dog' does not bite; the concept 'cock' does not crow. So Hume and Kant translate the fact of causation into the crude juxtaposition of two phenomena. Later authors, wishing to mitigate the crudeness, resolve the adjacency, whenever they can, into identity: cause and effect must be the same reality in disguise, and our perception of difference in these successions thus becomes an illusion. Lotze elaborately establishes that the 'influencing' of one thing by another is inconceivable. 'Influence' is a concept, and, as such, a distinct third thing, to be identified neither with the agent nor the patient. What becomes of it on its way from the former to the latter? And when it finds the latter, how does it act upon it? By a second influence which it puts forth in turn? — But then again how? and so forth, and so forth till our whole intuition of activity gets branded as illusory because you cannot possibly reproduce its flowing substance by juxtaposing the discrete. Intellectualism draws the dynamic continuity out of nature as you draw the thread out of a string of beads.

Example 2. *Knowledge is impossible;* for knower is one concept, and known is another. Discrete, separated by a chasm, they are mutually 'transcendent' things, so that how an

object can ever get into a subject, or a subject
ever get at an object, has become the most
unanswerable of philosophic riddles. An insin-
cere riddle, too, for the most hardened 'epis-
temologist' never really doubts that knowledge somehow does come off.

Example 3. *Personal identity is conceptually
impossible.* 'Ideas' and 'states of mind' are
discrete concepts, and a series of them in time
means a plurality of disconnected terms. To
such an atomistic plurality the associationists
reduce our mental life. Shocked at the discontinuous character of their scheme, the spiritu-
alists assume a 'soul' or 'ego' to melt the
separate ideas into one collective consciousness.
But this ego itself is but another discrete concept; and the only way not to pile up more
puzzles is to endow it with an incomprehensible power of producing that very character of
manyness-in-oneness of which rationalists refuse the gift when offered in its immediate perceptual form.

Example 4. *Motion and change are impossible.* Perception changes pulsewise, but the

pulses continue each other and melt their bounds. In conceptual translation, however, a continuum can only stand for elements with other elements between them *ad infinitum*, all separately conceived; and such an infinite series can never be exhausted by successive addition. From the time of Zeno the Eleatic, this intrinsic contradictoriness of continuous change has been one of the worst skulls at intellectualism's banquet.

Example 5. *Resemblance, in the way in which we naïvely perceive it, is an illusion.* Resemblance must be *defined;* and when defined it reduces to a mixture of identity with otherness. To know a likeness understandingly we must be able to abstract the identical point distinctly. If we fail of this, we remain in our perceptual limbo of 'confusion.'

Example 6. *Our immediate life is full of the sense of direction, but no concept of the direction of a process is possible until the process is completed.* Defined as it is by a beginning and an ending, a direction can never be prospectively but only retrospectively known. Our perceptual discernment beforehand of the way we are going, and all our dim foretastes of the future, have therefore to be treated as inexplicable or illusory features of experience.

Example 7. *No real thing can be in two relations at once;* the same moon, for example, cannot be seen both by you and by me. For the concept 'seen by you' is not the concept 'seen by me'; and if, taking the moon as a grammatical subject and, predicating one of these concepts of it, you then predicate the other also, you become guilty of the logical sin of saying that a thing can both be A and not-A at once. Learned trifling again; for clear though the conceptual contradictions be, nobody sincerely disbelieves that two men see the same thing.

Example 8. *No relation can be comprehended or held to be real in the form in which we innocently assume it.* A relation is a distinct concept; and when you try to make two other concepts continuous by putting a relation between them, you only increase the discontinuity. You have now conceived three things instead

SOME PROBLEMS OF PHILOSOPHY

of two, and have two gaps instead of one to bridge over. Continuity is impossible in the conceptual world.

Example 9. *The very relation of subject to predicate in our judgments, the backbone of conceptual thinking itself, is unintelligible and self-contradictory.* Predicates are ready-made universal ideas by which we qualify perceptual singulars or other ideas. Sugar, for example, we say 'is' sweet. But if the sugar was *already* sweet, you have made no step in knowledge; whilst if not so already, you are identifying it with a concept, with which, in its universality, the particular sugar cannot be identical. Thus neither the sugar as described, nor your description, is comprehensible.[1]

[1] I have cited in the text only such conceptual puzzles as have become classic in philosophy, but the concepts current in physical science have also developed mutual oppugnancies which (although not yet classic commonplaces in philosophy) are beginning to make physicists doubt whether such notions develop unconditional 'truth.' Many physicists now think that the concepts of 'matter,' 'mass,' 'atom,' 'ether,' 'inertia,' 'force,' etc. are not so much duplicates of hidden realities in nature as mental instruments to handle nature by after-substitution of their scheme. They are considered, like the kilogram or the imperial yard, 'artefacts,' not revelations. The literature here is copious: J. B. Stallo's *Concepts and Theories of Modern Physics* (1882); pp. 136–140 especially, are fundamental. Mach, Ostwald, Pearson

PERCEPT AND CONCEPT

These profundities of inconceivability, and many others like them, arise from the vain

Attitude of philosophers to the 'dialectic' difficulties attempt to reconvert the manifold into which our conception has resolved things, back into the continuum out of which it came. The concept 'many' is not the concept 'one'; therefore the manyness-in-oneness which perception offers is impossible to construe intellectually. Youthful readers will find such difficulties too whimsical to be taken seriously; but since the days of the Greek sophists these dialectic puzzles have lain beneath the surface of all our thinking like the shoals and snags in the Mississippi river; and the more intellectually conscientious the thinkers have been, the less they have allowed themselves to disregard them. But most philosophers have noticed this or that puzzle only, and ignored the others. The pyrrhonian Sceptics first, then Hegel,[1] then in our day Bradley and Bergson, are the only writers I know who have faced them col-

Duhem, Milhaud, LeRoy, Wilbois, H. Poincaré, are other critics of a similar sort.

[1] I omit Herbart, perhaps wrongly.

lectively, and proposed a solution applicable to them all.

The sceptics gave up the whole notion of truth light-heartedly, and advised their pupils The scep- not to care about it.[1] Hegel wrote so tics and Hegel abominably that I cannot understand him, and will say nothing about him here.[2] Bradley and Bergson write with beautiful clearness and their arguments continue all that I have said.

Mr. Bradley agrees that immediate feeling possesses a native wholeness which conceptual Bradley treatment analyzes into a many, but on per- cannot unite again. In every 'this' cept and concept as merely felt, Bradley says, we 'encounter' reality, but we encounter it only as a fragment, see it, as it were, only 'through a

[1] See any history of philosophy, *sub voce* 'Pyrrho.'

[2] Hegel connects immediate perception with ideal truth by a ladder of intermediary concepts — at least, I suppose they are concepts. The best opinion among his interpreters seems to be that ideal truth does not abolish immediate perception, but preserves it as an indispensable 'moment.' Compare, e. g., H. W. Dresser: *The Philosophy of the Spirit,* 1908; Supplementary Essay: 'On the Element of Irrationality in the Hegelian Dialectic.' In other words Hegel does not pull up the ladder after him when he gets to the top, and may therefore be counted as a non-intellectualist, in spite of his desperately intellectualist *tone.*

hole.'[1] Our sole practicable way of extending
and completing this fragment is by using our
intellect with its universal ideas. But with ideas,
that harmonious compenetration of manyness-
in-oneness which feeling originally gave is no
longer possible. Concepts indeed extend our
this, but lose the inner secret of its wholeness;
when ideal 'truth' is substituted for 'reality'
the very nature of 'reality' disappears.

The fault being due entirely to the conceptual form in which we have to think things, one
might naturally expect that one who recognizes
its inferiority to the perceptual form as clearly
as Mr. Bradley does, would try to save both
forms for philosophy, delimiting their scopes,
and showing how, as our experience works,
they supplement each other. This is M. Bergson's procedure; but Bradley, though a traitor
to orthodox intellectualism in holding fast to
feeling as a revealer of the inner oneness of
reality, has yet remained orthodox enough to
refuse to admit immediate feeling into 'philosophy' at all. 'For worse or for better,' he

---

[1] F. H. Bradley: *The Principles of Logic*, book i, chap. ii, pp. 29-32.

writes, the man who stays on particular feeling must remain outside philosophy.' The philosopher's business, according to Mr. Bradley, is to qualify the real 'ideally' (i. e. by concepts), and never to look back. The 'ideas' meanwhile yield nothing but a patchwork, and show no unity like that which the living perception gave. What shall one do in these perplexing circumstances? Unwilling to go back, Bradley only goes more desperately forward. He makes a flying leap ahead, and assumes, beyond the vanishing point of the whole conceptual perspective, an 'absolute' reality, in which the coherency of feeling and the completeness of the intellectual ideal shall unite in some indescribable way. Such an absolute totality-in unity *can* be, it *must* be, it *shall* be, it *is* he says. Upon this incomprehensible metaphysical object the Bradleyan metaphysic establishes its domain.[1]

The sincerity of Bradley's criticisms has cleared the air of metaphysics and made havoc

[1] Mr. Bradley has expressed himself most pregnantly in an article in volume xviii, N. S. of *Mind*, p. 489. See also his *Appearance and Reality, passim*, especially the Appendix to the second edition.

with old party lines. But, critical as he is, Mr. Bradley preserves one prejudice uncriti-

Criticism of Bradley

cized. Perception 'untransmuted,' he believes, must not, cannot, shall not, enter into final 'truth.'

Such loyalty to a blank direction in thought, no matter where it leads you, is pathetic: concepts disintegrate — no matter, their way must be pursued; percepts are integral — no matter, they must be left behind. When anti-sensationalism has become an obstinacy like this, one feels that it draws near its end.

Since it is only the conceptual form which forces the dialectic contradictions upon the innocent sensible reality, the remedy would seem to be simple. Use concepts when they help, and drop them when they hinder understanding; and take reality bodily and integrally up into philosophy in exactly the perceptual shape in which it comes. The aboriginal flow of feeling sins only by a quantitative defect. There is always much-at-once of it, but there is never enough, and we desiderate the rest. The only way to get the rest without wading through all

future time in the person of numberless per-
ceivers, is to substitute our various conceptual
systems which, monstrous abridgments though
they be, are nevertheless each an equivalent,
for some partial aspect of the full perceptual
reality which we can never grasp.

This, essentially, is Bergson's view of the
matter, and with it I think that we should rest
content.[1]

I will now sum up compendiously the result
of what precedes. If the aim of philosophy
Summary   were the taking full possession of all
reality by the mind, then nothing short of
the whole of immediate perceptual experience
could be the subject-matter of philosophy, for
only in such experience is reality intimately
and concretely found. But the philosopher,
although he is unable as a finite being to compass more than a few passing moments of such
experience, is yet able to extend his knowledge
beyond such moments by the ideal symbol of

---

[1] Bergson's most compendious statement of his doctrine is in the
'Introduction à la Métaphysique,' in the *Revue de Métaphysique et de
Morale*, 1903, p. i. For a brief comparison between him and Bradley,
see an essay by W. James, in the *Journal of Philosophy*, vol. vii, no. 2.

the other moments.[1] He thus commands vicariously innumerable perceptions that are out of range. But the concepts by which he does this, being thin extracts from perception, are always insufficient representatives thereof; and, although they yield wider information, must never be treated after the rationalistic fashion, as if they gave a deeper quality of truth. The deeper features of reality are found only in perceptual experience. Here alone do we acquaint ourselves with continuity, or the immersion of one thing in another, here alone with self, with substance, with qualities, with activity in its various modes, with time, with cause, with change, with novelty, with tendency, and with freedom. Against all such features of reality the method of conceptual translation, when candidly and critically followed out, can only raise its *non possumus*, and brand them as unreal or absurd.

[1] It would seem that in 'mystical' ways, he may extend his vision to an even wider perceptual panorama than that usually open to the scientific mind. I understand Bergson to favor some such idea as this See W. James: 'A Suggestion about Mysticism,' *Journal of Philosophy*, vii, 4. The subject of mystical knowledge, as yet very imperfectly understood, has been neglected both by philosophers and scientific men.

CHAPTER VI

PERCEPT AND CONCEPT — SOME COROLLARIES

THE first corollary of the conclusions of the foregoing chapter is that *the tendency known in philosophy as empiricism, becomes confirmed.* Empiricism proceeds from parts to wholes, treating the parts as fundamental both in the order of being and in the order of our knowledge.[1] In human experience the parts are per-

1. Novelty becomes possible

cepts, built out into wholes by our conceptual additions. The percepts are singulars that change incessantly and never return exactly as they were before. This brings an element of concrete novelty into our experience. This novelty finds no representation in the conceptual method, for concepts are abstracted from experiences already seen or given,

---

[1] Naturally this applies in the present place only to the greater whole which philosophy considers; the universe namely, and its parts, for there are plenty of minor wholes (animal and social organisms, for example) in which both the being of the parts and our understanding of the parts are founded.

and he who uses them to divine the new can never do so but in ready-made and ancient terms. Whatever actual novelty the future may contain (and the singularity and individuality of each moment makes it novel) escapes conceptual treatment altogether. Properly speaking, concepts are post-mortem preparations, sufficient only for retrospective understanding; and when we use them to define the universe prospectively we ought to realize that they can give only a bare abstract outline or approximate sketch, in the filling out of which perception must be invoked.

Rationalistic philosophy has always aspired to a rounded-in view of the whole of things, a closed system of kinds, from which the notion of essential novelty being possible is ruled out in advance. For empiricism, on the other hand, reality cannot be thus confined by a conceptual ring-fence. It overflows, exceeds, and alters. It may turn into novelties, and can be known adequately only by following its singularities from moment to moment as our experience grows. Empiricist philosophy thus renounces the pretension to an all-inclusive vision. It ekes out the narrowness of personal experience by concepts which it finds useful but not sovereign; but it stays inside the flux of life expectantly, recording facts, not formulating laws, and never pretending that man's relation to the totality of things as a philosopher is essentially different from his relation to the parts of things as a daily patient or agent in the practical current of events. Philosophy, like life, must keep the doors and windows open.

In the remainder of this book we shall hold fast to this empiricist view. We shall insist that, as reality is created temporally day by day, concepts, although a magnificent sketchmap for showing us our bearings, can never fitly supersede perception, and that the 'eternal' systems which they form should least of all be regarded as realms of being to know which is a kind of knowing that casts the knowledge of particulars altogether into the shade. That rationalist assumption is quite beside the mark. Thus does philosophy prove again that essential identity with science which we argued for in our first chapter.[1]

The last paragraph does not mean that concepts and the relations between them are not just as 'real' in their 'eternal' way as percepts are in their temporal way. What is it to be 'real'? The best definition I know is that which the pragmatist rule gives: 'anything is real of which we find ourselves obliged to take account in any way.'[2] Concepts are thus as real as percepts, for we cannot live a moment without taking account of them. But the 'eternal' kind of being which they enjoy is inferior to the temporal kind, because it is so static and schematic and lacks so many characters which temporal reality possesses. Philosophy must thus recognize many realms of reality

2. Conceptual systems are distinct realms of reality

---

[1] One way of stating the empiricist contention is to say that the 'alogical' enters into philosophy on an equal footing with the 'logical.' Mr. Belfort Bax, in his book, *The Roots of Reality* (1907), formulates his empiricism (such as it is) in this way. (See particularly chap. iii.) Compare also E. D. Fawcett: *The Individual and Reality, passim*, but especially part ii, chaps. iv and v.

[2] Prof. A. E. Taylor gives this pragmatist definition in his *Elements of Metaphysics* (1903), p. 51. On the nature of logical reality, cf. B. Russell: *Principles of Mathematics*.

which mutually interpenetrate. The conceptual systems of mathematics, logic, æsthetics, ethics, are such realms, each strung upon some peculiar form of relation, and each differing from perceptual reality in that in no one of them is history or happening displayed. Perceptual reality involves and contains all these ideal systems, and vastly more besides.

A concept, it was said above, means always the same thing: Change means always change, white always white, a circle always a circle. On this self-sameness of conceptual objects the static and 'eternal' character of our systems of ideal truth is based; for a relation, once perceived to obtain, must obtain always, between terms that do not alter. But many persons find difficulty in admitting that a concept used in different contexts can be intrinsically the same. When we call both snow and paper 'white' it is supposed by these thinkers that there must be two predicates in the field. As James Mill says:[1] 'Every colour is an individual colour,

3. The self-sameness of ideal objects

---

[1] *Analysis of the Human Mind* (1869), i, 249.

every size is an individual size, every shape is an individual shape. But things have no individual colour in common, no individual shape in common; no individual size in common; that is to say, they have neither shape, colour, nor size in common. What, then, is it which they have in common which the mind can take into view? Those who affirmed that it was something, could by no means tell. They substituted words for things; using vague and mystical phrases, which, when examined, meant nothing.' The truth, according to this nominalist author, is that the only thing that can be possessed in common by two objects is the same *name*. Black in the coat and black in the shoe are the same in so far forth as both shoe and coat are called black — the fact that on this view the name can never twice be the 'same' being quite overlooked. What now does the concept 'same' signify? Applying, as usual, the pragmatic rule, we find that when we call two objects the same we mean either (a) that no difference can be found between them when compared, or (b) that we can substitute the one for the other in certain operations without changing the result. If we are to discuss sameness profitably we must bear these pragmatic meanings in mind.

Do then the snow and the paper show no difference in color? And can we use them indifferently in operations? They may certainly replace each other for reflecting light, or be used indifferently as backgrounds to set off anything dark, or serve as equally good samples of what the word 'white' signifies. But the snow may be dirty, and the paper pinkish or yellowish without ceasing to be called 'white'; or both snow and paper in one light may differ from their own selves in another and still be 'white,' — so the no-difference criterion seems to be at fault. This physical difficulty (which all house painters know) of matching two tints so exactly as to show no difference seems to be the sort of fact that nominalists have in mind when they say that our ideal meanings are never twice the same. Must we therefore admit that such a concept as 'white' can never keep exactly the same meaning?

It would be absurd to say so, for we know that under all the modifications wrought by changing light, dirt, impurity in pigment, etc., there is an element of color-quality, different from other color-qualities, which we mean that our word *shall* inalterably signify. The impossibility of isolating and fixing this quality physically is irrelevant, so long as we can isolate and fix it mentally, and decide that whenever we say 'white,' that identical quality, whether applied rightly or wrongly, is what we shall be held to mean. Our meanings can be the same as often as we intend to have them so, quite irrespective of whether what is meant be a physical possibility or not. Half the ideas we make use of are of impossible or problematic things, — zeros, infinites, fourth dimensions, limits of ideal perfection, forces, relations sundered from their terms, or terms defined only conceptually, by their relations to other terms which may be equally fictitious. 'White' means a color quality of which the mind appoints the standard, and which it can decree to be there under all physical disguises. *That*

white is always the same white. What sense
can there be in insisting that although we ourselves have fixed it as the same, it cannot be
the same twice over? It works perfectly for
us on the supposition that it is there self-
identically; so the nominalist doctrine is false
of things of that conceptual sort, and true only
of things in the perceptual flux.

What I am affirming here is the platonic
doctrine that concepts are singulars, that concept-stuff is inalterable, and that physical
realities are constituted by the various con-
cept-stuffs of which they 'partake.' It is known
as 'logical realism' in the history of philosophy;
and has usually been more favored by rationalistic than by empiricist minds. For rationalism, concept-stuff is primordial and perceptual
things are secondary in nature. The present
book, which treats concrete percepts as primordial and concepts as of secondary origin,
may be regarded as somewhat eccentric in its
attempt to combine logical realism with an
otherwise empiricist mode of thought.[1]

[1] For additional remarks in favor of the sameness of conceptual ob-

PERCEPT AND CONCEPT

I mean by this that they are made of the same kind of stuff, and melt into each other

4. Concepts and percepts are consubstantial when we handle them together. How could it be otherwise when the concepts are like evaporations out of the bosom of perception, into which they condense again whenever practical service summons them? No one can tell, of the things he now holds in his hand and reads, how much comes in through his eyes and fingers, and how much, from his apperceiving intellect, unites with that and makes of it this particular 'book'? The universal and the particular parts of the experience are literally immersed in each other, and both are indispensable. Conception is not like a painted hook, on which no real chain can be hung; for we hang concepts upon percepts, and percepts upon concepts interchangeably and indefinitely; and the relation of the two is much more like what we find in those cylindrical 'panoramas'

jects, see W. James in *Mind*, vol. iv, 1879, pp. 331–335; F. H. Bradley: *Ethical Studies* (1876), pp. 151–154, and *Principles of Logic* (1883), pp. 260 ff., 282 ff. The nominalist view is presented by James Mill, as above, and by John Stuart Mill in his *System of Logic*, 8th ed. i, 77.

in which a painted background continues a real foreground so cunningly that one fails to detect the joint. The world we practically live in is one in which it is impossible, except by theoretic retrospection, to disentangle the contributions of intellect from those of sense. They are wrapt and rolled together as a gunshot in the mountains is wrapt and rolled in fold on fold of echo and reverberative clamor. Even so do intellectual reverberations enlarge and prolong the perceptual experience which they envelop, associating it with remoter parts of existence. And the ideas of these in turn work like those resonators that pick out partial tones in complex sounds. They help us to decompose our percept into parts and to abstract and isolate its elements.

The two mental functions thus play into each other's hands. Perception prompts our thought, and thought in turn enriches our perception. The more we see, the more we think; while the more we think, the more we see in our immediate experiences, and the greater grows the detail and the more significant the

articulateness of our perception.[1]   Later, when
we come to treat of causal activity, we shall see
how practically momentous is this enlargement
of the span of our knowledge through the wrap-
ping of our percepts in ideas.   It is the whole
coil and compound of both by which effects are
determined, and they may then be different
effects from those to which the perceptual
nucleus would by itself give rise.   But the point
is a difficult one and at the present stage of our
argument this brief mention of it must suffice.

Readers who by this time agree that our conceptual systems are secondary and on the
5. An ob-   whole imperfect and ministerial forms
jection
replied to   of being, will now feel able to return
and embrace the flux of their hourly experience
with a hearty feeling that, however little of it
at a time be given, what is given is absolutely

[1] Cf. F. C. S. Schiller: ' Thought and Immediacy,' in the *Journal
of Philosophy*, etc., iii, 234. The interpretation goes so deep that
we may even act as if experience consisted of nothing but the
different kinds of concept-stuff into which we analyze it. Such
concept-stuff may often be treated, for purposes of action and even
of discussion, as if it were a full equivalent for reality. But it is
needless to repeat, after what precedes, that no amount of it can
ever be a *full* equivalent, and that in point of genesis it remains a
secondary formation.

real. Rationalistic thought, with its exclusive interest in the unchanging and the general, has always de-realized the passing pulses of our life. It is no small service on empiricism's part to have exorcised rationalism's veto, and reflectively justified our instinctive feeling about immediate experience. 'Other world?' says Emerson, 'there is no other world,' — than this one, namely, in which our several biographies are founded.

> 'Natur hat weder Kern noch Schale;
> Alles ist sie mit einem male.
> Dich prüfe du nur allermeist,
> Ob du Kern oder Schale seist.'

The belief in the genuineness of each particular moment in which we feel the squeeze of this world's life, as we actually do work here, or work is done upon us, is an Eden from which rationalists seek in vain to expel us, now that we have criticized their state of mind.

But they still make one last attempt, and charge us with self-stultification.

'Your belief in the particular moments,' they insist, 'so far as it is based on reflective argument (and is not a mere omission to doubt, like that of cows and horses) is grounded in abstraction and conception. Only by using concepts have you established percepts in reality. The concepts are the vital things, then, and the percepts are dependent on them for the character of "reality" with which your reasoning endows them. You stand self-contradicted: concepts appear as the sole triumphant instruments of truth, for you have to employ their proper authority, even when seeking to install perception in authority above them.'

The objection is specious; but it disappears the moment one recollects that in the last resort a concept can only be *designative;* and that the concept 'reality,' which we restore to immediate perception, is no new conceptual creation, but only a kind of practical relation to our Will, *perceptively experienced,*[1] which reasoning had temporarily interfered with, but which, when the reasoning was neutralized by still further reasoning, reverted to its

[1] Compare W. James: *Principles of Psychology,* chap. xxi, " The Perception of Reality.'

original seat as if nothing had happened. That concepts can neutralize other concepts is one of their great practical functions. This answers also the charge that it is self-contradictory to use concepts to undermine the credit of conception in general. The best way to show that a knife will not cut is to try to cut with it. Rationalism itself it is that has so fatally undermined conception, by finding that, when worked beyond a certain point, it only piles up dialectic contradictions.[1]

[1] Compare further, as to this objection, a note in W. James: *A Pluralistic Universe*, pp. 339–343.

CHAPTER VII

THE ONE AND THE MANY

THE full nature, as distinguished from the full amount, of reality, we now believe to be given only in the perceptual flux. But, though the flux is continuous from next to next, non-adjacent portions of it are separated by parts that intervene, and such separation seems in a variety of cases to work a positive disconnection. The latter part, e. g., may contain no element surviving from the earlier part, may be unlike it, may forget it, may be shut off from it by physical barriers, or whatnot. Thus Pluralism vs. monism when we use our intellect for cutting up the flux and individualizing its members, we have (provisionally and practically at any rate) to treat an enormous number of these as if they were unrelated or related only remotely, to one another. We handle them piecemeal or distributively, and look at the entire flux as if it were their sum or collection. This encourages the empiricist notion,

113

that the parts are distinct and that the whole is a resultant.

This doctrine rationalism opposes, contending that the whole is fundamental, that the parts derive from it and all belong with one-another, that the separations we uncritically accept are illusory, and that the entire universe, instead of being a sum, is the only genuine unit in existence, constituting (in the words often quoted from d'Alembert) '*un seul fait et une grande vérité.*'

The alternative here is known as that between pluralism and monism. It is the most pregnant of all the dilemmas of philosophy, although it is only in our time that it has been articulated distinctly. Does reality exist distributively? or collectively? — in the shape of *eaches, everys, anys, eithers?* or only in the shape of an *all* or *whole?* An identical content is compatible with either form obtaining, the Latin *omnes*, or *cuncti*, or the German *alle* or *sämmtliche* expressing the alternatives familiarly. Pluralism stands for the distributive, monism for the collective form of being.

114

Please note that pluralism need not be supposed at the outset to stand for any particular kind or amount of disconnection between the many things which it assumes. It only has the negative significance of contradicting monism's thesis that there is absolutely *no* disconnection. The irreducible outness of *any*thing, however infinitesimal, from *any*thing else, in *any* respect, would be enough, if it were solidly established, to ruin the monistic doctrine.

I hope that the reader begins to be pained here by the extreme vagueness of the terms I am using. To say that there is 'no disconnection,' is on the face of it simply silly, for we find practical disconnections without number. My pocket is disconnected with Mr. Morgan's bank-account, and King Edward VII's mind is disconnected with this book. Monism must mean that all such apparent disconnections are bridged over by some deeper absolute union in which it believes, and this union must in some way be more real than the practical separations that appear upon the surface.

In point of historical fact monism has gen-

erally kept itself vague and mystical as regards
the ultimate principle of unity. To be One is
Kinds of
monism more wonderful than to be many, so
the principle of things must be One,
but of that One no exact account is given.
Plotinus simply calls it the One. 'The One is
all things and yet no one of them. . . . For
the very reason that none of them was in the
One, are all derived from it. Furthermore, in
order that they may be real existences, the One
Mystical
monism is not an existence, but the father
of existences. And the generation of
existence is as it were the first act of generation. Being perfect by reason of neither
seeking nor possessing nor needing anything,
the One overflows, as it were, and what overflows forms another hypostasis. . . . How
should the most perfect and primal good
stay shut up in itself as if it were envious or
impotent? . . . Necessarily then something
comes from it.'[1]

This is like the Hindoo doctrine of the Brah-

[1] Compare the passages in C. M. Bakewell's *Source-Book in Ancient
Philosophy*, pp. 363–370, or the first four books of the Vth Ennead
generally, in F. Bouillier's translation.

man, or of the Âtman. In the Bhagavat-gita the holy Krishna speaking for the One, says: 'I am the immolation. I am the sacrificial rite. I am the libation offered to ancestors. I am the drug. I am the incantation. I am the sacrificial butter also. I am the fire. I am the incense. I am the father, the mother, the sustainer, the grandfather of the universe — the mystic doctrine, the purification, the syllable "Om" . . . the path, the supporter, the master, the witness, the habitation, the refuge, the friend, the origin, the dissolution, the place, the receptacle, the inexhaustible seed. I heat (the world) I withhold and pour out the rain. I am ambrosia and death, the existing and the non-existing. . . . I am the same to all beings. I have neither foe nor friend. . . . Place thy heart on me, worshipping me, sacrificing to me, saluting me.'[1]

I call this sort of monism mystical, for it not only revels in formulas that defy understanding,[2] but it accredits itself by appealing to states of illumination not vouchsafed to com-

---

[1] J. C. Thomson's translation, chap. iv.

[2] Al-Ghazzali, the Mohammedan philosopher and mystic, gives a more theistic version of essentially the same idea: 'Allah is the guider

mon men. Thus Porphyry, in his life of Plotinus, after saying that he himself once had such an insight, when 68 years old, adds that whilst he lived with Plotinus, the latter four times had the happiness of approaching the supreme God and consciously uniting with him in a real and ineffable act.

The regular mystical way of attaining the vision of the One is by ascetic training, fundamentally the same in all religious systems. But this ineffable kind of Oneness is not strictly philosophical, for philosophy is essentially talkative and explicit, so I must pass it by.

The usual philosophic way of reaching deeper oneness has been by the conception of substance. First used by the Greeks, this notion

aright and the leader astray; he does what he wills and decides what he wishes; there is no opposer of his decision and no repeller of his decree. He created the Garden, and created for it a people, then used them in obedience. And he created the Fire, and created for it a people, then used them in rebellion. . . . Then he said, as has been handed down from the Prophet: "These are in the Garden, and I care not; and these are in the Fire, and I care not." So he is Allah, the Most High, the King, the Reality. He is not asked concerning what he does; but they are asked.' (D. B. MacDonald's translation, in *Hartford Seminary Record*, January, 1910.) Compare for other quotations, W. James: *The Varieties of Religious Experience*, pp. 415–422.

was elaborated with great care during the Middle Ages. Defined as any being that exists

Monism of substance per se, so that it needs no further subject in which to inhere (*Ens ita per se existens, ut non indigeat alio tamquam subjecto, cui inhaereat, ad existendum*) a 'substance' was first distinguished from all 'accidents' (which do require such a subject of inhesion — *cujus esse est inesse*). It was then identified with the 'principle of individuality' in things, and with their 'essence,' and divided into various types, for example into first and second, simple and compound, complete and incomplete, specific and individual, material and spiritual substances. God, on this view, is a substance, for he exists *per se*, as well as *a se;* but of secondary beings, he is the creator, not the substance, for once created, they also exist *per se* though not *a se.* Thus, for scholasticism, the notion of substance is only a partial unifier, and in its totality, the universe forms a pluralism from the substance-point-of-view.[1]

[1] Consult the word 'substance' in the index of any scholastic manual, such as J. Rickaby: *General Metaphysics;* A. Stöckl: *Lehrbuch d. Phil.;* or P. M. Liberatore: *Compendium Logicæ et Metaphysicæ.*

Spinoza broke away from the scholastic doctrine. He began his 'Ethics' by demonstrating that only one substance is possible, and that that substance can only be the infinite and necessary God.[1] This heresy brought reproba-

---

[1] Spinoza has expressed his doctrine briefly in part i of the Appendix to his *Ethics:* 'I have now explained,' he says, 'the nature of God, and his properties; such as that he exists necessarily; that he is unique; that what he is and does flows from the sole necessity of his nature; that he is the free cause of all things whatever; that all things are in God and depend on him in such wise that they can neither be nor be conceived without him; and finally, that all things have been predetermined by God, not indeed by the freedom of his will, or according to his good pleasure, but in virtue of his absolute nature or his infinite potentiality.' — Spinoza goes on to refute the vulgar notion of *final causes.* God pursues no ends — if he did he would lack something. He acts out of the logical necessity of the fulness of his nature. — I find another good monistic statement in a book of the spinozistic type: —
'. . . The existence of every compound object in manifestation does not lie in the object itself, but lies in the universal existence which is an absolute unit, containing in itself all that is manifested. All the particularized beings, therefore, . . . are incessantly changing one into the other, coming and going, forming and dissolving through the one universal cause of the *potential universe,* which is the absolute unit of universal existence, depending on the one general law, the one mathematical bond, which is the absolute being, and it changes not in all eternity. Thus, . . . it is the universe as a whole, *in its potential being,* from which the physical universe is individualized; and its being is a mathematical inference from a mathematical or an intellectual universe which was and ever is previously formed by an intellect standing and existing by itself. This mathematical or intellectual universe I call Absolute Intellectuality, the God of the Universe.'
(Solomon J. Silberstein: *The Disclosures of the Universal Mysteries,* New York, 1906, pp. 12-13.)

tion on Spinoza, but it has been favored by philosophers and poets ever since. The pantheistic spinozistic unity was too sublime a prospect not to captivate the mind. It was not till Locke, Berkeley, and Hume began to put in their 'critical' work that the suspicion began to gain currency that the notion of substance might be only a word masquerading in the shape of an idea.[1]

Locke believed in substances, yet confessed that 'we have no such clear idea at all, but only Critique of sub- stance an uncertain supposition of we know not what, which we take to be the substratum, or support of those ideas we do not know.'[2] He criticized the notion of personal substance as the principles of self-same-

[1] No one believes that such words as 'winter,' 'army,' 'house,' denote substances. They designate collective facts, of which the parts are held together by means that can be experimentally traced. Even when we can't define what groups the effects together, as in 'poison,' 'sickness,' 'strength,' we don't assume a substance, but are willing that the word should designate some phenomenal agency yet to be found out. Nominalists treat all substances after this analogy, and consider 'matter,' 'gold,' 'soul,' as but the names of so many grouped properties, of which the bond of union must be, not some unknowable substance corresponding to the name, but rather some hidden portion of the whole phenomenal fact.

[2] *Essay concerning Human Understanding*, book i, chap. iv, § 18.

ness in our different minds. *Experientially*, our personal identity consists, he said, in nothing more than the functional and perceptible fact that our later states of mind continue and remember our earlier ones.[1]

Berkeley applied the same sort of criticism to the notion of bodily substance. 'When I consider,' he says, 'the two parts ("being" in general, and "supporting accidents") which make the signification of the words "material substance," I am convinced there is no distinct meaning annexed to them. . . . Suppose an intelligence without the help of external bodies to be affected with the same train of sensations that you are, imprinted in the same order, and with like vividness in his mind. I ask whether that intelligence hath not all the reason to believe the existence of corporeal substances, represented by his ideas, and exciting them in his mind, that you can possibly have for believing the same thing.'[2] Certain *grouped sensations*, in short, are all that corporeal sub-

[1] Ibid., book ii, chap. xxvii, §§ 9–27.
[2] *Principles of Human Knowledge*, part i, §§ 17, 20.

stances are *known-as*, therefore the only meaning which the word 'matter' can claim is that it denotes such sensations and their groupings. They are the only verifiable aspect of the word.

The reader will recognize that in these criticisms our own pragmatic rule is used. What difference in practical experience is it supposed to make that we have each a personal substantial principle? This difference, that we can remember and appropriate our past, calling it 'mine.' What difference that in this book there is a substantial principle? This, that certain optical and tactile sensations cling permanently together in a cluster. The fact that certain perceptual experiences do seem to *belong together* is thus all that the word substance means. Hume carries the criticism to the last degree of clearness. 'We have no idea of substance,' he says, 'distinct from that of a collection of particular qualities, nor have we any other meaning when we either talk or reason concerning it. The idea of a substance . . . is nothing but a collection of simple ideas that are united by the imagination and have a particular name assigned them by which we are able to recall that collection.'[1] Kant's treatment of substance agrees with Hume's in denying all positive content to the notion. It differs in insisting that, by attaching shifting percepts to the permanent name, the category of substance unites them *necessarily* together, and thus makes nature intelligible.[2] It is impossible to assent to this. The grouping of qualities becomes no more intelligible when you call substance a 'category' than when you call it a bare word.

Let us now turn our backs upon ineffable or unintelligible ways of accounting for the world's oneness, and inquire whether, instead of being a principle, the 'oneness' affirmed may not merely be a name like 'substance,' descriptive of the fact that certain *specific and verifiable connections* are found among the parts of the experiential flux. This

Pragmatic analysis of oneness

---

[1] *Treatise on Human Nature*, part 1, § 6.

[2] *Critique of Pure Reason:* First Analogy of Experience. For further criticism of the substance-concept see J. S. Mill: *A System of Logic*, book i, chap. iii, §§ 6–9; B. P. Bowne: *Metaphysics*, part 1, chap. i. Bowne uses the words being and substance as synonymous.

brings us back to our pragmatic rule: Suppose there is a oneness in things, what may it be known-as? What differences to you and me will it make?

Our question thus turns upside down, and sets us on a much more promising inquiry. We can easily conceive of things that shall have no connection whatever with each other. We may assume them to inhabit different times and spaces, as the dreams of different persons do even now. They may be so unlike and in-commensurable, and so inert towards one an-other, as never to jostle or interfere. Even now there may actually be whole universes so dis-parate from ours that we who know ours have no means of perceiving that they exist. We con-ceive their diversity, however; and by that fact the whole lot of them form what is known in logic as one 'universe of discourse.' To form a universe of discourse argues, as this example shows, no further kind of connection. The im-portance attached by certain monistic writers to the fact that any chaos may become a uni-verse by being merely named, is to me incomprehensible. We must seek something better in the way of oneness than this susceptibility of being mentally considered together, and named by a collective noun.

What connections may be perceived concretely or in point of fact, among the parts of the collection abstractly designated as our 'world'?

There are innumerable modes of union among its parts, some obtaining on a larger, some on a smaller scale. Not all the parts of our world are united *mechanically*, for some can move without the others moving. They all seem united by *gravitation*, however, so far as they are material things. Some again Kinds of oneness of these are united *chemically*, while others are not; and the like is true of thermic, optical, electrical, and other *physical* connections. These connections are specifications of what we mean by the word oneness when we apply it to our world. We should not call it one unless its parts were connected in these and other ways. But then it is clear that by the same logic we ought to call it 'many' so far as its parts are disconnected in these same ways, chemically inert towards one another or non-conductors to electricity, light and heat. In all these modes of union, some parts of the world prove to be conjoined with other parts, so that if you choose your line of influence and your items rightly, you may travel from pole to pole without an interruption. If, however, you choose them wrongly, you meet with obstacles and non-conductors from the outset, and cannot travel at all. There is thus neither absolute oneness nor absolute manyness from the physical point of view, but a mixture of well-definable modes of both. Moreover, neither the oneness nor the manyness seems the more essential attribute, they are co-ordinate features of the natural world.

There are plenty of other practical differences meant by calling a thing One. Our world, being strung along in time and space, has *temporal and spatial unity*. But time and space relate things by determinately sundering them, so it is hard to say whether the world ought

more to be called 'one' or 'many' in this spatial
or temporal regard.

The like is true of the *generic oneness* which
comes from so many of the world's parts being
similar. When two things are similar you can
make inferences from the one which will hold
good of the other, so that this kind of union
among things, so far as it obtains, is inexpres-
sibly precious from the logical point of view.
But an infinite heterogeneity among things
exists alongside of whatever likeness of kind
we discover; and our world appears no more
distinctly or essentially as a One than as a
Many, from this generic point of view.

We have touched on the noetic unity pre-
dicable of the world in consequence of our
being able to mean the whole of it at once.
Widely different from unification by an abstract designation, would be the concrete noetic
union wrought by an all-knower of perceptual
type who should be acquainted at one stroke
with every part of what exists. In such an absolute all-knower idealists believe. Kant, they
say, virtually replaced the notion of Substance,

by the more intelligible notion of Subject. The 'I am conscious of it,' which on some witness's part must accompany every possible experience, means in the last resort, we are told, one individual witness of the total frame of things, world without end, amen. You may call his undivided act of omniscience instantaneous or eternal, whichever you like, for time is its object just as everything else is, and itself is not in time.

We shall find reasons later for treating noetic monism as an unverified hypothesis. Over Unity by against it there stands the noetic concate- nation pluralism which we verify every moment when we seek information from our friends. According to this, everything in the world might be known by somebody, yet not everything by the same knower, or in one single cognitive act, — much as all mankind is knit in one network of acquaintance, A knowing B, B knowing C, — Y knowing Z, and Z possibly knowing A again, without the possibility of anyone knowing everybody at once. This 'concatenated' knowing, going from next to next, is altogether different from the 'consolidated' knowing supposed to be exercised by the absolute mind. It makes a coherent type of universe in which the widest knower that exists may yet remain ignorant of much that is known to others.

There are other systems of concatenation besides the noetic concatenation. We ourselves are constantly adding to the connections of things, organizing labor-unions, establishing postal, consular, mercantile, railroad, telegraph, colonial, and other systems that bind us and things together in ever wider reticulations. Some of these systems involve others, some do not. You cannot have a telephone system without air and copper connections, but you can have air and copper connections without telephones. You cannot have love without acquaintance, but you can have acquaintance without love, etc. The same thing, moreover, can belong to many systems, as when a man is connected with other objects by heat, by gravitation, by love, and by knowledge.

From the point of view of these partial systems, the world hangs together from next to next in a variety of ways, so that when you are off of one thing you can always be on to something else, without ever dropping out of your world. Gravitation is the only positively known sort of connection among things that reminds us of the consolidated or monistic form of union. If a 'mass' should change anywhere, the mutual gravitation of all things would instantaneously alter.

Teleological and æsthetic unions are other forms of systematic union. The world is full Unity of of partial purposes, of partial stories. purpose, meaning That they all form chapters of one supreme purpose and inclusive story is the monistic conjecture. They *seem*, meanwhile, simply to run alongside of each other — either irrelevantly, or, where they interfere, leading to mutual frustrations, — so the appearance of things is invincibly pluralistic from this purposive point of view.

It is a common belief that all particular beings have one origin and source, either in God, or in atoms all equally old. There is no real novelty, it is believed, in the universe, Unity of the new things that appear having origin either been eternally prefigured in the absolute, or being results of the same *primordia rerum*, atoms, or monads, getting into new mixtures. But the question of being is so obscure anyhow, that whether realities have burst into existence all at once, by a single 'bang,' as it were; or whether they came piecemeal, and have different ages (so that real novelties may be leaking into our universe all the time), may here be left an open question, though it is undoubtedly intellectually economical to suppose that all things are equally old, and that no novelties leak in.

These results are what the Oneness of the Universe is *known-as*. They *are* the oneness, Summary pragmatically considered. A world coherent in any of these ways would be no chaos, but a universe of such or such a grade. (The grades might differ, however. The parts, e. g., might have space-relations, but nothing more; or they might also gravitate; or exchange heat; or know, or love one another, etc.)

Such is the cash-value of the world's unity, empirically realized. Its total unity is the sum of all the partial unities. It consists of them and follows upon them. Such an idea, however, outrages rationalistic minds, which habitually despise all this practical small-change. Such minds insist on a deeper, more through-and-through union of all things in the absolute, 'each in all and all in each,' as the prior condition of these empirically ascertained connections. But this may be only a case of the usual worship of abstractions, like calling 'bad weather' the cause of to-day's rain, etc., or accounting for a man's features by his 'face,' when really the rain *is* the bad weather, is what you *mean* by 'bad weather,' just as the features are what you mean by the face.

To sum up, the world is 'one' in some respects, and 'many' in others. But the respects must be distinctly specified, if either statement is to be more than the emptiest abstraction. Once we are committed to this soberer view, the question of the One or the Many may well cease to appear important. The amount either of unity or of plurality is in short only a matter for observation to ascertain and write down, in statements which will have to be complicated, in spite of every effort to be concise.

CHAPTER VIII[1]

THE ONE AND THE MANY (*continued*) — VALUES AND DEFECTS

W<small>E</small> might dismiss the subject with the preceding chapter[2] were it not for the fact that further consequences follow from the rival hypotheses, and make of the alternative of monism or pluralism what I called it on page 114, the most 'pregnant' of all the dilemmas of metaphysics.

To begin with, the attribute 'one' seems for many persons to confer a value, an ineffable

The monistic theory

illustriousness and dignity upon the world, with which the conception of it as an irreducible 'many' is believed to clash.

Secondly, a through-and-through noetic connection of everything with absolutely everything else is in some quarters held to be indispensable to the world's rationality. Only then might we believe that all things really do

---

[1] [This chapter was not indicated as a separate chapter in the manuscript. E<small>D</small>.]

[2] For an amplification of what precedes, the lecture on 'The One and the Many ' in W. James: *Pragmatism* (1907), may be referred to.

belong together, instead of being connected by the bare conjunctions 'with' or 'and.' The notion that this latter pluralistic arrangement may obtain is deemed 'irrational'; and of course it does make the world partly alogical or non-rational from a purely intellectual point of view.

Monism thus holds the oneness to be the more vital and essential element. The entire cosmos must be a consolidated unit, within which each member is determined by the whole to be just that, and from which the slightest incipiency of independence anywhere is ruled out. With Spinoza, monism likes to believe that all things follow from the essence of God as necessarily as from the nature of a triangle it follows that the angles are equal to two right angles. The whole is what yields the parts, not the parts the whole. The universe is *tight*, monism claims, not loose; and you must take the irreducible whole of it just as it is offered, or have no part or lot in it at all. The only alternative allowed by monistic writers is to confess the

The value of absolute oneness

world's non-rationality — and no philosopher can permit himself to do that. The form of monism regnant at the present day in philosophic circles is *absolute idealism*. For this way of thinking, the world exists no otherwise than as the object of one infinitely knowing mind. The analogy that suggests the hypothesis here is that of our own finite fields of consciousness, which at every moment envisage a much-at-once composed of parts related variously, and in which both the conjunctions and the disjunctions that appear are there only in so far as we are there as their witnesses, so that they are both 'noetically' and monistically based.

We may well admit the sublimity of this noetic monism and of its vague vision of an underlying connection among all phenomena without exception.[1] It shows itself also able to confer religious stability and peace, and it invokes the authority of mysticism in its favor. Yet, on the other hand, like many another con-

[1] In its essential features, Spinoza was its first prophet, Fichte and Hegel were its middle exponents, and Josiah Royce is its best contemporary representative.

cept unconditionally carried out, it introduces
Its defects into philosophy puzzles peculiar to
itself, as follows: —

1. It does not account for our finite consciousness. If nothing exists but as the Absolute Mind knows it, how can anything exist
otherwise than as that Mind knows it? That
Mind knows each thing in one act of knowledge, along with every other thing. Finite
minds know things without other things, and
this ignorance is the source of most of their
woes. We are thus not simply objects to an all-
knowing subject: we are subjects on our own
account and know differently from its knowing.

2. It creates a problem of evil. Evil, for pluralism, presents only the practical problem of
how to get rid of it. For monism the puzzle is
theoretical: How — if Perfection be the source,
should there be Imperfection? If the world
as known to the Absolute be perfect, why
should it be known otherwise, in myriads of
inferior finite editions also? The perfect edition surely was enough. How do the breakage
and dispersion and ignorance get in?

3. It contradicts the character of reality as perceptually experienced. Of our world, change seems an essential ingredient. There is history. There are novelties, struggles, losses, gains. But the world of the Absolute is represented as unchanging, eternal, or 'out of time,' and is foreign to our powers either of apprehension or of appreciation. Monism usually treats the sense-world as a mirage or illusion.

4. It is fatalistic. Possibility, as distinguished from necessity on the one hand and from impossibility on the other, is an essential category of human thinking. For monism, it is a pure illusion; for whatever is is necessary, and aught else is impossible, if the world be such a unit of fact as monists pretend.

Our sense of 'freedom' supposes that some things at least are decided here and now, that the passing moment may contain some novelty, be an original starting-point of events, and not merely transmit a push from elsewhere. We imagine that in some respects at least the future may not be co-implicated with the past, but may be really addable to it, and indeed addable in one shape *or* another, so that the next turn in events can at any given moment genuinely be ambiguous, i. e., possibly this, but also possibly that.

Monism rules out this whole conception of possibles, so native to our common-sense. The future and the past are linked, she is obliged to say; there can be no genuine novelty anywhere, for to suppose that the universe has a constitution simply additive, with nothing to link things together save what the words 'plus,' 'with,' or 'and' stand for, is repugnant to our reason.

Pluralism, on the other hand, taking perceptual experience at its face-value, is free from all these difficulties. It protests against working our ideas in a vacuum made of conceptual abstractions. Some parts of our world, it admits, cannot exist out of their wholes; but The plu- others, it says, can. To some extent ralistic theory the world *seems* genuinely additive: it may really be so. We cannot explain conceptually *how* genuine novelties can come; but if one did come we could experience *that* it came.

140

We do, in fact, experience perceptual novelties all the while. Our perceptual experience overlaps our conceptual reason: the *that* transcends the *why*. So the common-sense view of life, as something really dramatic, with work done, and things decided here and now, is acceptable to pluralism. 'Free will' means nothing but real novelty; so pluralism accepts the notion of free will.

But pluralism, accepting a universe unfinished, with doors and windows open to possibilities uncontrollable in advance, gives us less religious certainty than monism, with its absolutely closed-in world. It is true that monism's religious certainty is not rationally based, but is only a faith that 'sees the All-Good in the All-Real.' In point of fact, however, monism is usually willing to exert this optimistic faith: its world is certain to be saved, yes, is saved already, unconditionally and from eternity, in spite of all the phenomenal appearances of risk.[1]

[1] For an eloquent expression of the monistic position, from the religious point of view, read J. Royce: *The World and the Individual*, vol. ii, lectures 8, 9, 10.

A world working out an uncertain destiny,

Its de-
fects
as the phenomenal world appears
to be doing, is an intolerable idea
to the rationalistic mind.

Pluralism, on the other hand, is neither optimistic nor pessimistic, but melioristic, rather. The world, it thinks, may be saved, on condition that its parts shall do their best. But shipwreck in detail, or even on the whole, is among the open possibilities.

There is thus a practical lack of balance about pluralism, which contrasts with monism's peace of mind. The one is a more moral, the other a more religious view; and different men usually let this sort of consideration determine their belief.[1]

So far I have sought only to show the respective implications of the rival doctrines without

Its ad-
vantages
dogmatically deciding which is the
more true. It is obvious that pluralism has three great advantages:—

1. It is more 'scientific,' in that it insists

---

[1] See, as to this religious difference, the closing lecture in W. James's *Pragmatism*.

that when oneness is predicated, it shall mean definitely ascertainable conjunctive forms. With these the disjunctions ascertainable among things are exactly on a par. The two are co-ordinate aspects of reality. To make the conjunctions more vital and primordial than the separations, monism has to abandon verifiable experience and proclaim a unity that is indescribable.

2. It agrees more with the moral and dramatic expressiveness of life.

3. It is not obliged to stand for any particular amount of plurality, for it triumphs over monism if the smallest morsel of disconnectedness is once found undeniably to exist. 'Ever not quite' is all it says to monism; while monism is obliged to prove that what pluralism asserts can in no amount whatever possibly be true — an infinitely harder task.

The advantages of monism, in turn, are its natural affinity with a certain kind of religious faith, and the peculiar emotional value of the conception that the world is a unitary fact.

So far has our use of the pragmatic rule brought us towards understanding this dilemma. The reader will by this time feel for himself the essential practical difference which it involves. The word 'absence' seems to indicate it. The monistic principle implies that nothing that is can in any way whatever be absent from anything else that is. The pluralistic principle, on the other hand, is quite compatible with some things being absent from operations in which other things find themselves singly or collectively engaged. *Which* things are absent from which other things, and *when*, — these of course are questions which a pluralistic philosophy can settle only by an exact study of details. The past, the present, and the future in perception, for example, are absent from one another, while in imagination they are present or absent as the case may be. If the time-content of the world be not one monistic block of being, if some part, at least, of the future, is added to the past without being virtually one therewith, or implicitly contained therein, then it is absent really as well as phenomenally and may be called an absolute novelty in the world's history in so far forth.

Towards this issue, of the reality or unreality of the novelty that appears, the pragmatic

Monism, pluralism, and novelty

difference between monism and pluralism seems to converge. That we ourselves may be authors of genuine novelty is the thesis of the doctrine of free-will. That genuine novelties can occur means that from the point of view of what is already given, what comes may have to be treated as a matter of *chance*. We are led thus to ask the question: In what manner does new being come? Is it through and through the consequence of older being or is it matter of chance so far as older being goes? — which is the same thing as asking: Is it original, in the strict sense of the word?

We connect again here with what was said at the end of Chapter III. We there agreed that being is a datum or gift and has to be begged by the philosopher; but we left the question open as to whether he must beg it all at once or beg it bit by bit or in instalments. The latter is the more consistently empiricist view, and I shall begin to defend it in the chapter that follows.

CHAPTER IX

THE PROBLEM OF NOVELTY

THE impotence to explain being which we have attributed to all philosophers is, it will be recollected, a conceptual impotence. It is when thinking abstractly of the whole of being at once, as it confronts us ready-made, that we feel our powerlessness so acutely. Possibly, if we followed the empiricist method, considering the parts rather than the whole, and imagining ourselves inside of them perceptually, the subject might defy us less provokingly. We are thus brought back to the problem with which Chapter VII left off. When perceptible amounts of new phenomenal being come to birth, must we hold them to be in all points predetermined and necessary outgrowths of the being already there, or shall we rather admit the possibility that originality may thus instil itself into reality?

If we take concrete perceptual experience, the question can be answered in only one way. 'The same returns not, save to bring the dif-

ferent.' Time keeps budding into new moments, every one of which presents a content

Percept-   which in its individuality never was
ual nov-
elty   before and will never be again. Of

no concrete bit of experience was an exact du-
plicate ever framed. 'My youth,' writes Delbœuf, 'has it not taken flight, carrying away
with it love, illusion, poetry, and freedom from
care, and leaving with me instead science, aus-
tere always, often sad and morose, which sometimes I would willingly forget, which repeats to
me hour by hour its grave lessons, or chills me
by its threats? Will time, which untiringly piles
deaths on births, and births on deaths, ever re-
make an Aristotle or an Archimedes, a Newton
or a Descartes? Can our earth ever cover itself
again with those gigantic ferns, those immense
equisetaceans, in the midst of which the same
antediluvian monsters will crawl and wallow
as they did of yore? . . . No, what has been
will not, cannot, be again. Time moves on
with an unfaltering tread, and never strikes
twice an identical hour. The instants of which
the existence of the world is composed are all

dissimilar, — and whatever may be done, something remains that can never be reversed.'[1]

The everlasting coming of concrete novelty into being is so obvious that the rationalizing intellect, bent ever on explaining what is by what was, and having no logical principle but identity to explain by, treats the perceptual flux as a phenomenal illusion, resulting from the unceasing re-combination in new forms of mixture, of unalterable elements, coeval with the world. These elements are supposed to be the only real beings; and, for the intellect once grasped by the vision of them, there can be nothing genuinely new under the sun. The world's history, according to molecular science, signifies only the 'redistribution' of the unchanged atoms of the primal firemist, parting and meeting so as to appear to us spectators in the infinitely diversified configurations which we name as processes and things.[2]

Science and novelty

[1] J. Delbœuf: *Revue Philosophique*, vol. ix, p. 138 (1880). On the infinite variety of reality, compare also W. T. Marvin: *An Introduction to Systematic Philosophy*, New York, 1903, pp. 22–30.

[2] The Atomistic philosophy, which has proved so potent a scientific instrument of explanation, was first formulated by Democritus, who

So far as physical nature goes few of us experience any temptation to postulate real novelty. The notion of eternal elements and their mixture serves us in so many ways, that we adopt unhesitatingly the theory that primordial being is inalterable in its attributes as well as in its quantity, and that the laws by which we describe its habits are uniform in the strictest mathematical sense. These are the absolute conceptual foundations, we think,

died 370 B. C. His life overlapped that of Aristotle, who took what on the whole may be called a biological view of the world, and for whom 'forms' were as real as elements. The conflict of the two modes of explanation has lasted to our day, for some chemists still defend the Aristotelian tradition which the authority of Descartes had interrupted for so long, and deny our right to say that 'water' is not a simple entity, or that oxygen and hydrogen atoms persist in it unchanged. Compare W. Ostwald: *Die Ueberwindung des wissenschaftlichen Materialismus* (1895), p. 12: 'The atomistic view assumes that when in iron-oxide, for example, all the sensible properties both of iron and oxygen have vanished, iron and oxygen are nevertheless there but now manifest other properties. We are so used to this assumption that it is hard for us to feel its oddity, nay, even its absurdity. When, however, we reflect that all we know of a given kind of matter is its properties, we realize that the assertion that the matter is still there, but without any of those properties, is not far removed from nonsense.' Compare the same author's *Principles of Inorganic Chemistry*, English translation, 2d ed. (1904), p. 149 f. Also P. Duhem: 'La Notion de Mixte,' in the *Revue de Philosophie*, vol. i, p. 452 ff. (1901). — The whole notion of the eternal fixity of elements is melting away before the new discoveries about radiant matter. See for radical statements G. Le Bon: *L'Évolution de la Matière*.

spread beneath the surface of perceptual variety. It is when we come to human lives, that

Personal experience and novelty our point of view changes. It is hard to imagine that 'really' our own subjective experiences are only molecular arrangements, even though the molecules be conceived as beings of a psychic kind. A material fact may indeed be different from what we feel it to be, but what sense is there in saying that a feeling, which has no other nature than to be felt, is not as it *is* felt? Psychologically considered, our experiences resist conceptual reduction, and our fields of consciousness, taken simply as such, remain just what they appear, even though facts of a molecular order should prove to be the signals of the appearance. Biography is the concrete form in which all that is is immediately given; the perceptual flux is the authentic stuff of each of our biographies, and yields a perfect effervescence of novelty all the time. New men and women, books, accidents, events, inventions, enterprises, burst unceasingly upon the world. It is vain to resolve these into ancient ele-

SOME PROBLEMS OF PHILOSOPHY

ments, or to say that they belong to ancient kinds, so long as no one of them in its full individuality ever was here before or will ever come again. Men of science and philosophy, the moment they forget their theoretic abstractions, live in their biographies as much as any one else, and believe as naïvely that fact even now is making, and that they themselves, by doing 'original work,' help to determine what the future shall become.

I have already compared the live or perceptual order with the conceptual order from this point of view. Conception knows no way of explaining save by deducing the identical from the identical, so if the world is to be conceptually rationalized no novelty can really come. This is one of the traits in that general bankruptcy of conceptualism, which I enumerated in Chapter V — conceptualism can *name* change and growth, but can translate them into no terms of its own, and is forced to contradict the indestructible sense of life within us by denying that reality grows.

It may seem to the youthful student a rather

'far cry' from the question of the possibility of novelty to the 'problem of the infinite,' but in the history of speculation, the two problems have been connected. Novelty seems to violate continuity; continuity seems to involve

Novelty and the infinite 'infinitely' shaded gradation; infinity connects with number; and number with fact in general — for facts have to be numbered. It has thus come to pass that the nonexistence of an infinite number has been held to necessitate the finite character of the constitution of fact; and along with this its discontinuous genesis, or, in other words, its coming into being by discrete increments of novelty however small.

Thus we find the problem of the infinite already lying across our path. It will be better at this point to interrupt our discussion of the more enveloping question of novelty at large, and to get the minor problem out of our way first. I turn then to the problem of the infinite.

CHAPTER X

NOVELTY AND THE INFINITE — THE CONCEPTUAL VIEW [1]

The problem is as to which is the more rational supposition, that of continuous or that of discontinuous additions to whatever amount or kind of reality already exists.

On the discontinuity-theory, time, change, etc., would grow by finite buds or drops, either nothing coming at all, or certain units of amount bursting into being 'at a stroke.' Every feature of the universe would on this view have a finite numerical constitution. Just as atoms, not half- or quarter-atoms are the minimum of matter that can be, and every finite amount of matter contains a finite number of atoms, so any amounts of time, space, change, etc., which we might assume would be composed of a finite number of minimal amounts of time, space, and change.

Such a discrete composition is what actually

The discontinuity-theory

---

[1] [In the author's manuscript this chapter and the succeeding chapters were labelled 'sub-problems,' and this chapter was entitled 'The Continuum and the Infinite.' Ed.]

obtains in our perceptual experience. We either perceive nothing, or something already there in sensible amount. This fact is what in psychology is known as the law of the 'threshold.' Either your experience is of no content, of no change, or it is of a perceptible amount of content or change. Your acquaintance with reality grows literally by buds or drops of perception. Intellectually and on reflection you can divide these into components, but as immediately given, they come totally or not at all.

If, however, we take time and space as concepts, not as perceptual data, we don't well see how they can have this atomistic constitution. For if the drops or atoms are themselves without duration or extension it is inconceivable that by adding any number of them together times or spaces should accrue.

The continuity theory

If, on the other hand, they are minute durations or extensions, it is impossible to treat them as real minima. Each temporal drop must have a later and an earlier half, each spatial unit a right and a left half, and these halves must themselves have halves, and so on *ad infinitum*, so that with the notion that the constitution of things is continuous and not discrete, that of a divisibility *ad infinitum* is inseparably bound up. This infinite divisibility of some facts, coupled with the infinite expansibility of others (space, time, and number) has given rise to one of the most obstinate of philosophy's dialectic problems. Let me take up, in as simple a way as I am able to, the *problem of the infinite*.

There is a pseudo-problem, 'How can the finite know the infinite?' which has troubled some English heads.[1] But one might as well make a problem of 'How can the fat know the lean?' When we come to treat of knowledge, such problems will vanish. The real problem of the infinite began with the famous arguments against motion, of Zeno the Eleatic. The school of Pythagoras was pluralistic. 'Things are numbers,' the master had said, meaning apparently that reality was made of

[1] In H. Calderwood's *Philosophy of the Infinite* one will find the subordinate difficulties discussed, with almost no consciousness shown of the important ones.

points which one might number.[1] Zeno's arguments were meant to show, not that motion could not really take place, but that it could not truly be conceived as taking place by the successive occupancy of points. If a flying **Zeno's** arrow occupies at each point of time **paradoxes** a determinate point of space, its motion becomes nothing but a sum of rests, for it exists not, out of any point; and *in* the point it does n't move. Motion cannot truly occur as thus discretely constituted.

Still better known than the 'arrow' is the 'Achilles' paradox. Suppose Achilles to race with a tortoise, and to move twice as fast as his rival, to whom he gives an inch of headstart. By the time he has completed that inch, or in other words advanced to the tortoise's starting point, the tortoise is half an inch ahead of him. While Achilles is traversing that half inch, the tortoise is traversing a quarter of an inch, etc. So that the successive points occupied by the runners simultane-

[1] I follow here J. Burnet: *Early Greek Philosophers* (the chapter on the Pythagoreans), and Paul Tannery: 'Le concept scientifique du continu' in the *Revue Philosophique*, xx, 385.

ously form a convergent series of distances from the starting point of Achilles. Measured in inches, these distances would run as follows:

$$1 + \tfrac{1}{2} + \tfrac{1}{4} + \tfrac{1}{8} + \tfrac{1}{16} \cdots \cdots + \tfrac{1}{n} \cdots \cdots \tfrac{1}{\infty}$$

Zeno now assumes that space must be infinitely divisible. But if so, then the number of points to be occupied cannot all be enumerated in succession, for the series begun above is interminable. Each time that Achilles gets to the tortoise's last point it is but to find that the tortoise has already moved to a further point; and although the interval between the points quickly grows infinitesimal, it is mathematically impossible that the two racers should reach any one point at the same moment. If Achilles could overtake the tortoise, it would be at the end of two inches; and if his speed were two inches a second, it would be at the end of the first second;[1] but the argument shows that he simply cannot overtake the animal. To do so would oblige him to exhaust,

[1] This shows how shallow is that common 'exposure' of Zeno's 'sophism,' which charges it with trying to prove that to overtake the tortoise, Achilles would require an infinitely long time.

by traversing one by one, the whole of them, a series of points which the law of their formation obliges to come never to an end.

Zeno's various arguments were meant to establish the 'Eleatic' doctrine of real being, which was monistic. The 'minima sensibilia' of which space, time, motion, and change consist for our perception are not real 'beings,' for they subdivide themselves *ad infinitum*. The nature of real being is to be entire or continuous. Our perception, being of a hopeless 'many,' thus is false.

Our own mathematicians have meanwhile constructed what they regard as an adequate continuum, composed of points or numbers. When I speak again of that I shall have occasion to return to the Achilles-fallacy, so called. At present I will pass without transition to the next great historic attack upon the problem of the infinite, which is the section on the 'Antinomies' in Kant's 'Critique of Pure Reason.'

Kant's views need a few points of preparation, as follows: —

1. That real or objective existence must be

determinate existence may be regarded as an axiom in ontology. We may be dim as to just how many stars we see in the Pleiades, or doubtful whose count to believe regarding them; but seeing and belief are subjective affections, and the stars by themselves, we are sure, exist in definite numbers. 'Even the hairs of our head are numbered,' we feel certain, though no man shall ever count them.[1] Any existent reality, taken in itself, must therefore be countable, and to any group of such realities some definite number must be applicable.

Kant's antinomies

2. Kant defines infinity as 'that which can never be completely measured by the successive addition of units' — in other words, as that which defies complete enumeration.

3. Kant lays it down as axiomatic that if anything is 'given,' as an existent reality, the whole sum of the 'conditions' required to account for it must similarly be given, or have been given. Thus if a cubic yard of space be

---

[1] Of the origin in our experience of this singularly solid postulate, I will say nothing here.

'given,' all its parts must equally be given. If a certain date in past time be real, then the previous dates must also have been real. If an effect be given, the whole series of its causes must have been given, etc., etc.

But the 'conditions' in these cases defy enumeration: the parts of space are less and less *ad infinitum*, times and causes form series that are infinitely regressive for our counting, and of no such infinite series can a 'whole' be formed. Any such series has a variable value, for the number of its terms is indefinite; whereas the conditions under consideration ought, if the 'whole sum of them' be really given, to exist (by the principle, 1, above) in fixed numerical amount.[1]

---

[1] The contradiction between the infinity in the *form* of the conditions, and the numerical determinateness implied in the *fact* of them, was ascribed by Kant to the 'antinomic' form of our experience. His solution of the puzzle was by the way of 'idealism,' and is one of the prettiest strokes in his philosophy. Since the conditions cannot exist in the shape of a totalized amount, it must be, he says, that they do not exist independently or *an sich*, but only as phenomena, or *for us*. Indefiniteness of amount is not incompatible with merely phenomenal existence. *Actual* phenomena, whether conditioned or conditioning, are there for us only in finite amount, as given to perception at any given moment; and the infinite form of them means only that we can go on perceiving, conceiving or imagining more and more about them,

Such was the form of the puzzle of the infinite, as Kant propounded it. The reader will observe a bad ambiguity in the statement. When he speaks of the 'absolute totality of the synthesis' of the conditions, the words suggest that a completed collection of them must exist or have existed. When we hear that 'the whole sum of them must be given,' we interpret it to mean that they must be given in the form of a whole sum, whereas all that the logical situation requires is that *no one of them should be lacking*, an entirely different demand, and one that can be gratified as well in an infinitely growing as in a terminated series. The same

Ambigu- things can always be taken either
ity of
Kant's collectively or distributively, can be
statement
of the talked of either as 'all,' or as 'each,'
problem or as 'any.' Either statement can be

applied equally well to what exists in finite

world without end. It does not mean that what we go on thus to represent shall have been there already by itself, apart from our acts of representation. Experience, for idealism, thus falls into two parts, a phenomenal given part which is finite, and a conditioning infinite part which is not given, but only possible to experience hereafter. Kant distinguishes this second part, as only *aufgegeben* (or set to us as a task), from the first part as *gegeben* (or already extant).

number; and 'all that is there' will be covered
both times. But things which appear under
the form of endless series can be talked of only
distributively, if we wish to leave none of them
out. When we say that 'any,' 'each,' or 'every'
one of Kant's conditions must be fulfilled, we
are therefore on impeccable ground, even
though the conditions should form a series as
endless as that of the whole numbers, to which
we are forever able to add one. But if we say
that 'all' must be fulfilled, and imagine 'all'
to signify a sum harvested and gathered-in,
and represented by a number, we not only
make a requirement utterly uncalled for by the
logic of the situation, but we create puzzles and
incomprehensibilities that otherwise would not
exist, and that may require, to get rid of them
again, hypotheses as violent as Kant's idealism.

In the works of Charles Renouvier, the
strongest philosopher of France during the
second half of the nineteenth century, the
problem of the infinite again played a pivotal
part. Starting from the principle of the nu-

merical determinateness of reality (supra, page 160) — the '*principe du nombre,*' as he called it — and recognizing that the series of numbers 1, 2, 3, 4, . . . etc., leads to no final 'infinite' number, he concluded that such reali-

<small>Renouvier's solution</small> ties as present beings, past events and causes, steps of change and parts of matter, must needs exist in limited amount. This made of him a radical pluralist. Better, he said, admit that being gives itself to us abruptly, that there are first beginnings, absolute numbers, and definite cessations, however intellectually opaque to us they may seem to be, than try to rationalize all this arbitrariness of fact by working-in explanatory conditions which would involve in every case the self-contradiction of things being paid-in and completed, although they are infinite in formal composition.

With these principles, Renouvier could believe in absolute novelties, unmeditated be-

<small>His solution favors novelty</small> ginnings, gifts, chance, freedom, and acts of faith. Fact, for him, overlapped; conceptual explanation fell short; real-

ity must in the end be begged piecemeal, not everlastingly deduced from other reality. This, the empiricist, as distinguished from the rationalist view, is the hypothesis set forth at the end of our last chapter.[1]

[1] I think that Renouvier made mistakes, and I find his whole philosophic manner and apparatus too scholastic. But he was one of the greatest of philosophic characters, and but for the decisive impression made on me in the seventies by his masterly advocacy of pluralism, I might never have got free from the monistic superstition under which I had grown up. The present volume, in short, might never have been written. This is why, feeling endlessly thankful as I do, I dedicate this text-book to the great Renouvier's memory. Renouvier's works make a very long list. The fundamental one is the *Essais de Critique Générale* (first edition, 1854–1864, is in four, second edition, 1875, in six volumes). Of his latest opinions *Le Personnalisme* (1903) gives perhaps the most manageable account; while the last chapter of his *Esquisse d'une Classification des Systèmes* (entitled 'Comment je suis arrivé à ces conclusions') is an autobiographic sketch of his dealings with the problem of the infinite. *Derniers entretiens*, dictated while dying, at the age of eighty-eight, is a most impressive document, coming as if from a man out of Plutarch.

CHAPTER XI[1]

NOVELTY AND THE INFINITE — THE PERCEPTUAL VIEW

K<small>ANT</small>'s and Renouvier's dealings with the infinite are fine examples of the way in which philosophers have always been wont to infer matters of fact from conceptual considerations. Real novelty would be a matter of fact; and so would be the idealistic constitution of experience;[2] but Kant and Renouvier deduce these facts from the purely logical impossibility of an infinite number of conditions getting completed. It seems a very short cut to truth; but if the logic holds firm, it may be a fair cut,[3] and the possibility obliges us to scrutinize the situation with increasing care. Proceeding so

[1] [This chapter was not indicated as a separate chapter in the manuscript. E<small>D</small>.]

[2] For an account of idealism the reader is referred to chapter below. [Never written. E<small>D</small>.]

[3] Let me now say that we shall ourselves conclude that change completed by steps infinite in number is inadmissible. This is hardly inferring fact from conceptual considerations, it is only concluding that a certain conceptual hypothesis regarding the fact of change will not work satisfactorily. The field is thus open for any other hypothesis; and the one which we shall adopt is simply that which the face of perceptual experience suggests.

to do, we immediately find that in the class of
infinitely conditioned things, we must distinguish two sub-classes, as follows: —

1. Things conceived as *standing*, like space,
past time, existing beings.

2. Things conceived as *growing*, like motion,
change, activity.

In the standing class there seems to be no
valid objection to admitting both real exist-

The stand- ence, and a numerical copiousness de-
ing in-
finite manding infinity for its description.
If, for instance, we consider the stars, and
assume the number of them to be infinite, we
need only suppose that to each several term of
the endless series 1, 2, 3, 4, ... n ..., there cor-
responds one star. The numbers, growing endlessly, would then never exceed the stars standing there to receive them. Each number would
find its own star waiting from eternity to be
numbered; and this *in infinitum*, some star
that ever was, matching each number that shall
be used. As there is no 'all' to the numbers so
there need be none to the stars. One cannot
well see how the existence of each star should

oblige the whole class 'star' to be of one number rather than of another, or require it to be
of any terminated number. What I say here
of stars applies to the component parts of
space and matter, and to those of past time.[1]

So long as we keep taking such facts piecemeal, and talk of them distributively as 'any'
Its prag-
matic
definition or 'each,' the existence of them in
infinite form offers no logical diffi-
culty. But there is a psychological tendency to
slip from the distributive to the collective way
of talking, and this produces a sort of mental
flicker and dazzle out of which the dialectic
difficulties emerge. 'If each condition be there,'
— we say, 'then all are there, for there cannot

---

[1] Past time may offer difficulty to the student as it has to better
men! It has terminated in the present moment, paid itself out and
made an 'amount.' But this amount can be counted in both directions;
and in both, one may think it ought to give the same result. If, when
counted forward, it came to an end in the present, then when counted
backward, it must, we are told, come to a like end in the past. It must
have had a beginning, therefore, and its amount must be finite. The
sophism here is gross, and amounts to saying that what has one bound
must have two. The 'end' of the forward counting *is* the 'beginning'
of the backward counting, and is the *only* beginning logically implied.
The ending of a series in no way prejudices the question whether it
were beginningless or not; and this applies as well to tracts of time as
to the abstract regression which 'negative' numbers form.

be eaches that do not make an all.' Rightly
taken, the phrase 'all are there,' means only
that 'not one is absent.' But in the mouths of
most people, it surreptitiously foists in the
wholly irrelevant notion of a bounded total.

There are other similar confusions. 'How,'
it may be asked, in Locke's words, can a
'growing measure' fail to overtake a 'standing
bulk'? And standing existence must some time
be overtaken by a growing number-series,
must be finished or finite in its numerical
determination. But this again foists in the
notion of a bound. What is given as 'standing'
in the cases under review is not a 'bulk,' but
each star, atom, past date or what not; and to
call these eaches a 'bulk,' is to beg the very
point at issue. But probably the real reason
why we object to a standing infinity is the
reason that made Hegel speak of it as the
'false' infinite. It is that the vertiginous chase
after ever more space, ever more past time,
ever more subdivision, seems endlessly stupid.
What need is there, what use is there, for so
much? Not that any amount of anything is

absolutely too big to be; but that some amounts are too big for our imagination to wish to caress them. So we fall back with a feeling of relief on some form or other of the finitist hypothesis.[1]

If now we turn from static to growing forms of being, we find ourselves confronted by much more serious difficulties. Zeno's and Kant's dialectic holds good wherever, before an end The growing in-finite can be reached, a succession of terms, endless by definition, must needs have been *successively* counted out. This is the case with every process of change, however small; with every event which we conceive as unrolling itself continuously. What is continuous must be divisible *ad infinitum;* and from division to division here you cannot proceed by addition (or by what Kant calls the succes-

[1] The reader will note how emphatically in all this discussion, I am insisting on the distributive or piecemeal point of view. The distributive is identical with the pluralistic, as the collective is with the monistic conception. We shall, I think, perceive more and more clearly as this book proceeds, that *piecemeal existence is independent of complete collectibility*, and that some facts, at any rate, exist only distributively, or in form of a set of eaches which (even if in infinite number) need not in any intelligible sense either experience themselves, or get experienced by anything else, as members of an All.

sive synthesis of units) and touch a farther limit. You can indeed define what the limit ought to be, but you cannot reach it *by this process*. That Achilles should occupy *in succession* 'all' the points in a single continuous inch of space, is as inadmissible a conception as that he should count the series of whole numbers 1, 2, 3, 4, etc., to infinity and reach an end. The terms are not 'enumerable' in that order; and the order it is that makes the whole difficulty. An infinite 'regression' like the rearward perspective of time offers no such contradiction, for it comes not in that order. Its 'end' is what we start with; and each successive note 'more' which our imagination has to add, *ad infinitum,* is thought of as already having been paid in and not as having yet to be paid before the end can be attained. Starting with our end, we have to wait for nothing. The infinity here is of the 'standing' variety. It is, in the word of Kant's pun, *gegeben*, not *aufgegeben:* in the other case, of a continuous process to be traversed, it is on the contrary *aufgegeben:* it is a task — not only for our philosophic imagination, but for any real agent who might try physically to compass the entire performance. Such an agent is bound by logic to find always a remainder, something ever yet to be paid, like the balance due on a debt with even the interest of which we do not catch up.

'*Infinitum in actu pertransiri nequit,*' said scholasticism; and every continuous quantum

The growing infinite must be treated as discontinuous

to be gradually traversed is conceived as such an infinite. The quickest way to avoid the contradiction would seem to be to give up that conception, and to treat real processes of change no longer as being continuous, but as taking place by finite not infinitesimal steps, like the successive drops by which a cask of water is filled, when whole drops fall into it at once or nothing. This is the radically pluralist, empiricist, or perceptualist position, which I characterized in speaking of Renouvier (above, pages 164–165). We shall have to end by adopting it in principle ourselves, qualifying it so as to fit it closely to perceptual experience.

Meanwhile we are challenged by a certain school of critics who think that what in mathe-

Objec-matics is called 'the new infinite'
tions
has quashed the old antinomies, and who treat anyone whom the notion of a completed infinite in any form still bothers, as a very *naïf* person. *Naïf* though I am in mathematics, I must, notwithstanding the dryness of the subject, add a word in rebuttal of these criticisms, some of which, as repeated by novices, tend decidedly towards mystification.

The 'new infinite' and the 'number-continuum' are outgrowths of a general attempt

(1) The to accomplish what has been called
number-
continuum the 'arithmetization' ($\grave{\alpha}\rho\iota\theta\mu\grave{o}s$ meaning number) of all quantity. Certain *quanta* (grades of intensity or other difference, amounts of space) have until recently been supposed to be immediate data of perceptive sensibility or 'intuition'; but philosophical mathematicians have now succeeded in getting a conceptual equivalent for them in the shape of collections of numbers created by interpolation between one another indefinitely. We can halve any

line in space, and halve its halves and so on. But between the cuts thus made and numbered, room is left for infinite others created by using 3 as a divisor, for infinite others still by using 5, 7, etc., until all possible 'rational' divisions of the line shall have been made. Between these it is now shown that interpolation of cuts numbered 'irrationally' is still possible *ad infinitum*, and that with these the line at last gets filled *full*, its continuity now being wholly translated into these numbered cuts, and their number being infinite. 'Of the celebrated formula that continuity means "unity in multiplicity," the multiplicity alone subsists, the unity disappears,'[1] — as indeed it does in all conceptual translations — and the original intuition of the line's extent gets treated, from the mathematical point of view, as a 'mass of uncriticized prejudice' by Russell, or sneered at by Cantor as a 'kind of religious dogma.'[2]

So much for the number-continuum. As for 'the new infinite': that means only a new defi-

---

[1] H. Poincaré: *La science et l'hypothese*, p. 30.
[2] B. Russell: *The Philosophy of Mathematics*, i, 260, 287.

nition of infinity. If we compare the indefi-
nitely-growing number-series, 1, 2, 3, 4, - - - n,
- - - in its entirety, with any component part of
(2) The   it, like 'even' numbers 'prime' num-
'new
infinite'   bers, or 'square' numbers, we are
confronted with a paradox. No one of the parts,
thus named, of the number-series, is equal to
the whole collectively taken; yet any one of
them is 'similar' to the whole, in the sense that
you can set up a one-to-one relation between
each of its elements and *each* element of the
whole, so that part and whole prove to be of
what logicians call the same 'class,' numerically. Thus, in spite of the fact that even numbers, prime numbers, and square numbers are
much fewer and rarer than numbers in general,
and only form a part of numbers *überhaupt*
they appear to be equally copious for purposes
of counting. The terms of each such partial
series can be numbered by using the natural
integers in succession. There is, for instance, a
first prime, a second prime, etc., *ad infinitum;*
and queerer-sounding still, since *every* integer,
odd or even, can be doubled, it would seem that

the even numbers thus produced cannot in the nature of things be less multitudinous than that series of both odd and even numbers of which the whole natural series consists.

These paradoxical consequences result, as one sees immediately, from the fact that the

The new infinite paradoxical

infinity of the number-series is of the 'growing' variety (above, page 170). They were long treated as a *reductio ad absurdum* of the notion that such a variable series spells infinity in act, or can ever be translated into standing or collective form.[1] But contemporary mathematicians have taken the bull by the horns. Instead of treating such paradoxical properties of indefinitely growing series as *reductiones ad absurdum*, they have turned them into the proper definition of infinite classes of things. Any class is now called

---

[1] The fact that, taken distributively, or paired each to each, the terms in one endlessly growing series should be made a match for those in another (or 'similar' to them) is quite compatible with the two series being collectively of vastly unequal amounts. You need only make the steps of difference, or distances, between the terms much longer in one series than in the other, to get numerically similar multitudes, with greatly unequal magnitudes of content. Moreover the moment either series should stop growing, the 'similarity' would cease to exist.

infinite if its parts are numerically similar to itself. If its parts are numerically dissimilar, it is finite. This definition now separates the conception of the class of finite from that of infinite objects.

Next, certain concepts, called 'transfinite numbers,' are now *created by definition*. They **'Trans-finite numbers'** are decreed to belong to the infinite class, and yet not to be formed by adding one to one *ad infinitum*, but rather to be postulated outright as coming *after each and all of the numbers formed by such addition.*[1] Cantor gives the name of 'Omega' to the lowest of these possible transfinite numbers. It would, for instance, be the number of the point at which Achilles overtakes the tortoise — if he does overtake him— by exhausting all the intervening points successively. Or it would be the number of the stars, in case their count-

[1] The class of all numbers that 'come before the first transfinite' is a definitely limited conception, provided we take the numbers as *eaches* or *anys*, for then any one and every of them will have by definition to come *before* the transfinite number comes — even though they form no whole and there be no last one of them, and though the transfinite have no immediate predecessor. The transfinite is, in a word, not an ordinal conception, at least it does not continue the order of entire numbers.

ing could not terminate. Or again it would be the number of miles away at which parallel lines meet — if they do meet. It is, in short, a 'limit' to the whole class of numbers that grow one by one, and like other limits, it proves a useful conceptual bridge for passing us from one range of facts to another.

The first sort of fact we pass to with its help is the number of the number-continuum **Their uses** or point-continuum described above **and de-** (page 173) as generated by infinitely **fects** repeated subdivision. The making of the subdivisions is an infinitely growing process; but the number of subdivisions that can be made has for its limit the transfinite number Omega just imagined and defined; thus is a growing assimilated to a standing multitude; thus is a number that is variable practically equated (by the process of passing to the limit) with one that is fixed; thus do we circumvent the law of indefinite addition, or division which previously was the only way in which infinity was constructable, and reach a constant infinite at a bound. This infinite number may now be substituted for any continuous finite quantum, however small the latter may perceptually appear to be.

When I spoke of my 'mystification,' just now, I had partly in mind the contemptuous way in which some enthusiasts for the 'new infinite' treat those who still cling to the superstition that 'the whole is greater than the part.' Because any point whatever in an imaginary inch is now conceivable as being matched by some point in a quarter-inch or half-inch, this numerical 'similarity' of the different *quanta*, taken point-wise, is treated as if it signified that half-inches, quarter-inches, and inches are mathematically identical things anyhow, and that their differences are facts which we may scientifically neglect. I may misunderstand the newest expounders of Zeno's famous 'sophism,' but what they say seems to me virtually to be equivalent to this.

Mr. Bertrand Russell (whom I do not accuse of mystification, for Heaven knows he tries to make things clear!) treats the Achilles-puzzle as if the difficulty lay only in seeing how the paths traversed by the two runners (measured after the race is run, and assumed then to con-

Russell's solution of Zeno's paradox by their means

sist of nothing but points of position coincident with points upon a common scale of time) should have the same time-measure if they be not themselves of the same length. But the two paths are of different lengths; for owing to the tortoise's head-start, the tortoise's path is only a part of the path of Achilles. How, then, if time-points are to be the medium of measurement, can the longer path *not* take the longer time?

The remedy, for Mr. Russell, if I rightly understand him, lies in noting that the sets of points in question are conceived as being infinitely numerous in both paths, and that where infinite multitudes are in question, to say that the whole is greater than the part is false. For each and every point traversed by the tortoise there is one point traversed by Achilles, at the corresponding point of time; and the exact correspondence, point by point, of either one of the three sets of points with both the others, makes of them similar and equally copious sets from the numerical point of view. There is thus no recurrent 'remainder' of the tortoise's head-start with which Achilles cannot catch up, which he can reduce indefinitely, but cannot annul. The books balance to the end. The last point in Achilles's path, the last point in the tortoise's, and the last time-instant in the race are terms which mathematically coincide. With this, which seems to be Mr. Russell's way of analyzing the situation, the puzzle is supposed to disappear.[1]

It seems to me however that Mr. Russell's statements dodge the real difficulty, which

The solution criticized

concerns the 'growing' variety of infinity exclusively, and not the 'standing' variety, which is all that he envisages when he assumes the race already to have been run and thinks that the only problem that remains is that of numerically equating the paths. The real difficulty may almost be

---

[1] Mr. Russell's own statements of the puzzle as well as of the remedy are too technical to be followed verbatim in a book like this. As he finds it necessary to paraphrase the puzzle, so I find it convenient to paraphrase him, sincerely hoping that no injustice has been done.

called physical, for it attends the process of *formation* of the paths. Moreover, two paths are not needed — that of either runner alone, or even the lapse of empty time, involves the difficulty, which is that of touching a goal when an interval needing to be traversed first keeps permanently reproducing itself and getting in your way. Of course the same quantum can be produced in various manners. This page which I am now painfully writing, letter after letter, will be printed at a single stroke. God, as the orthodox believe, created the space-continuum, with its infinite parts already standing in it, by an instantaneous *fiat*. Past time now stands in infinite perspective, and may conceivably have been created so, as Kant imagined, for our retrospection only, and all at once. 'Omega' was created by a single decree, a single act of definition in Prof. Cantor's mind. But whoso actually *traverses* a continuum, can do so by no process continuous in the mathematical sense. Be it short or long, each point must be occupied in its due order of succession; and if the points are necessarily infinite, their end cannot be reached, for the 'remainder,' in this kind of process, is just what one cannot 'neglect.' 'Enumeration' is, in short, the sole possible method of occupation of the series of positions implied in the famous race; and when Mr. Russell solves the puzzle by saying as he does, that 'the definition of whole and part without enumeration is the key to the whole mystery,'[1] he seems to me deliberately to throw away his case.[2]

---

[1] *The Philosophy of Mathematics*, i, 361. — Mr. Russell gives a *Tristram Shandy* paradox as a counterpart to the Achilles. Since it took T. S. (according to Sterne) two years to write the history of the first two days of his life, common sense would conclude that at that rate the life never could be written. But Mr. Russell proves the contrary; for, as days and years have no last term, and the *nth* day is written in the *nth* year, any assigned day will be written about, and no part of the life remain unwritten. But Mr. Russell's proof cannot be applied to the real world without the physical hypothesis which he expresses by saying: 'If Tristram Shandy lives forever, and does not weary of his task.' In all real cases of continuous change a similarly absurd hypothesis must be made: the agent of the change must live forever, in the sense of outliving an endless set of points of time, and 'not wearying' of his impossible task.

[2] Being almost blind mathematically and logically, I feel considerable shyness in differing from such superior minds, yet what can one do but follow one's own dim light? The literature of the new infinite is so technical that it is impossible to cite details of it in a non-mathematical work like this. Students who are interested should consult the tables of contents of B. Russell's *Philosophy of Mathematics*, of L. Couturat's *Infini Mathématique*, or his *Principes des Mathématiques*.

After this disagreeable polemic, I conclude that the new infinite need no longer block the way to the empiricist opinion which we reached provisionally on page 172. Irrelevant though they be to facts the 'conditions' of which are of the 'standing' sort, the criticisms of Leibnitz, Kant, Cauchy, Renouvier, Evellin and others, apply legitimately to all cases of supposedly continuous growth or change. The 'conditions' here have to be fulfilled seriatim; and if the series which they form were endless, its limit, if 'successive synthesis' were the only way of reaching it, could simply not be reached. Either we must

Conclusions

A still more rigorous exposition may be found in E. V. Huntington, *The Continuum as a Type of Order*, in the *Annals of Mathematics*, vols. vi and vii (reprint for sale at publication-office, Harvard University). Compare also C. S. Peirce's paper in the *Monist*, ii, 537–546, as well as the presidential address of E. W. Hobson in the *Proceedings of the London Mathematical Society*, vol. xxxv. For more popular discussions see J. Royce, *The World and the Individual*, vol. i, Supplementary Essay; Keyser: *Journal of Philosophy*, etc., i, 29, and *Hibbert Journal*, vii, 380–390; S. Waterton in *Aristotelian Soc. Proceedings*, 1910; Leighton: *Philosophical Review*, xiii, 497; and finally the tables of contents of H. Poincaré's three recent little books, *La science et l'hypothèse*, Paris ; *The Value of Science* (authorized translation by G. B. Halsted), New York, 1907 ; *Science et Méthode*, Paris, 1908. The liveliest short attack which I know upon infinites completed by successive synthesis, is that in G. M. Fullerton's *System of Metaphysics*, chapter xi.

stomach logical contradiction, therefore, in these cases; or we must admit that the limit is reached in these successive cases by finite and perceptible units of approach — drops, buds, steps, or whatever we please to term them, of change, coming wholly when they do come, or coming not at all. Such seems to be the nature of concrete experience, which changes always by sensible amounts, or stays unchanged. The infinite character we find in it is woven into it by our later conception indefinitely repeating the act of subdividing any given amount supposed. The facts do not resist the subsequent conceptual treatment; but we need not believe that the treatment necessarily reproduces the operation by which they were originally brought into existence.

The antinomy of mathematically continuous

1. Conceptual transformation of perceptual experience turns the infinite into a problem

growth is thus but one more of those many ways in which our conceptual transformation of perceptual experience makes it less comprehensible than ever. That being should immediately and by finite quantities add itself to being, may indeed be something which an onlooking intellect fails to understand; but that being should be identified with the consummation of an endless chain of units (such as 'points'), no one of which contains any amount whatever of the being (such as 'space') expected to result, this is something which our intellect not only fails to understand, but which it finds absurd. The substitution of 'arithmetization' for intuition thus seems, if taken as a description of reality, to be only a partial success. Better accept, as Renouvier says, the opaquely given data of perception, than concepts inwardly absurd.[1]

[1] The point-continuum illustrates beautifully my complaint that the intellectualist method turns the flowing into the static and discrete. The buds or steps of process which perception accepts as primal gifts of being, correspond logically to the 'infinitesimals' (minutest *quanta* of notion, change or what not) of which the latest mathematics is supposed to have got rid. Mr. Russell accordingly finds himself obliged, just like Zeno, to treat motion as an unreality: 'Weierstrass,' he says, 'by strictly banishing all infinitesimals has at last shown that we live in an unchanging world, and that the arrow, at every moment of its flight, is truly at rest' (*op. cit.*, p. 347). 'We must entirely reject the notion of a state of motion,' he says elsewhere; 'motion consists merely in the occupation of different places at different times. . . . There is no transition from place to place, no consecutive moment, or consecutive position, no such thing as velocity except in the sense of a real number which is the limit of a certain set of quotients' (p. 473). The mathematical 'continuum,' so called, becomes thus an absolute discontinuum in any physical or experiential sense. Ex-

NOVELTY AND THE INFINITE

So much for the 'problem of the infinite,' and for the interpretation of continuous change by the new definition of infinity. We find that the picture of a reality changing by steps finite in number and discrete, remains quite as acceptable to our understanding and as congenial to our imagination as before; so, after these dry and barren chapters, we take up our main topic of inquiry just where we had laid it down. Does reality grow by abrupt increments of novelty, or not? The contrast between discontinuity and continuity now confronts us in another form. The mathematical definition of continuous quantity as 'that between any two elements or terms of which there is another term' is directly opposed to the more empirical or perceptual notion that anything is continuous when its parts appear as immediate next neighbors, with absolutely nothing between.

2. It leaves the problem of novelty where it was

tremes meet; and although Russell and Zeno agree in denying perceptual motion, for the one a pure unity, for the other a pure multiplicity takes its place. It is probable that Russell's denial of change, etc. is meant to apply only to the mathematical world. It would be unfair to charge him with writing metaphysics in these passages, although he gives no warning that this may not be the case.

Our business lies hereafter with the perceptual account, but before we settle definitively to its discussion, another classic problem of philosophy had better be got out of the way. This is the 'problem of causation.'

CHAPTER XII[1]

NOVELTY AND CAUSATION — THE CONCEPTUAL VIEW

IF reality changes by finite sensible steps, the question whether the bits of it that come are radically new, remains unsettled still. Remember our situation at the end of Chapter III. Being *überhaupt* or at large, we there found to be undeduceable. For our *intellect* it remains a casual and contingent quantum that is simply found or begged. May it be begged bit by bit, as it adds itself? Or must we beg it only once, by assuming it either to be eternal or to have come in an instant that co-implicated all the rest of time? Did or did not 'the first morning of creation write what the last dawn of reckoning shall read'? With these questions monism and pluralism stand face to face again. The classic obstacle to pluralism has always been what is known as the 'principle of causality.' This principle has been

The 'principle of causality'

---

[1] [In the author's manuscript this chapter bore the heading — 'Second Sub-problem — Cause and Effect.' ED.]

taken to mean that the effect in some way already exists in the cause. If this be so, the effect cannot be absolutely novel, and in no radical sense can pluralism be true.

We must therefore review the facts of causation. I take them in conceptual translation before considering them in perceptual form. The first definite inquiry into causes was made by Aristotle.[1]

The 'why' of anything, he said, is furnished by four principles: the material cause of it (as Aristotle on causation when bronze makes a statue); the formal cause (as when the ratio of two to one makes an octave); the efficient cause (as when a father makes a child) and the final cause (as when one exercises for the sake of health). Christian philosophy adopted the four causes; but what one generally means by the cause of anything is its 'efficient' cause, and in what immediately follows I shall speak of that alone.

An efficient cause is scholastically defined as

[1] Book 2, or book 5, chap. ii of his *Metaphysics*, or chap. iii of his *Physics*, give what is essential in his views.

'that which produces something else by a real activity proceeding from itself.' This is unques-

Scholasti-cism on the efficient cause

tionably the view of common sense; and scholasticism is only common sense grown quite articulate. Passing over the many classes of efficient cause which scholastic philosophy specifies, I will enumerate three important sub-principles it is supposed to follow from the above definition. Thus: 1. No effect can come into being without a cause. This may be verbally taken; but if, avoiding the word effect, it be taken in the sense that nothing can happen without a cause, it is the famous 'principle of causality' which, when combined with the next two principles, is supposed to establish the block-universe, and to render the pluralistic hypothesis absurd.

2. The effect is always proportionate to the cause, and the cause to the effect.

3. Whatever is in the effect must in some way, whether formally, virtually, or eminently, have been also in the cause. ('Formally' here means that the cause resembles the effect, as

when one motion causes another motion; virtually means that the cause somehow involves that effect, without resembling it, as when an artist causes a statue but possesses not himself its beauty; 'eminently' means that the cause, though unlike the effect, is superior to it in perfection, as when a man overcomes a lion's strength by greater cunning.)

Nemo dat quod non habet is the real principle from which the causal philosophy flows; and the proposition *causa æquat effectum* practically sums up the whole of it.[1]

It is plain that each moment of the universe must contain all the causes of which the next moment contains effects, or to put it with extreme concision, it is plain that each moment in its totality causes the next moment.[2] But

---

[1] Read for a concise statement of the school-doctrine of causation the account in J. Rickaby: *General Metaphysics*, book 2, chap. iii. I omit from my text various subordinate maxims which have played a great part in causal philosophy, as 'The cause of a cause is the cause of its effects'; 'The same causes produce the same effects'; 'Causes act only when present'; 'A cause must exist before it can act,' etc.

[2] This notion follows also from the consideration of conditioning circumstances being at bottom as indispensable as causes for producing effects. 'The cause, philosophically speaking, is the sum total of the conditions positive and negative,' says J. S. Mill (*Logic*, 8th edition, i,

if the maxim holds firm that *quidquid est in effectu debet esse prius aliquo modo in causa*, it follows that the next moment can contain nothing genuinely original, and that the novelty that appears to leak into our lives so unremittingly, must be an illusion, ascribable to the shallowness of the perceptual point of view.

Scholasticism always respected common sense, and in this case escaped the frank denial of all genuine novelty by the vague qualification 'aliquo modo.' This allowed the effect also to differ, *aliquo modo*, from its cause. But conceptual necessities have ruled the situation and have ended, as usual, by driving nature and perception to the wall. A cause and its effect are two numerically discrete concepts, and yet in some inscrutable way the former must 'produce' the latter. How can it intelligibly do so, save by already hiding the latter in itself? Numerically two, cause and effect

383). This is equivalent to the entire state of the universe at the moment that precedes the effect. But neither is the 'effect' in that case the one fragmentary event which our attention first abstracted under that name. It is that fragment, along with all its concomitants — or in other words it is the entire state of the universe at the second moment desired.

must be generically one, in spite of the perceptual appearances; and causation changes thus from a concretely experienced relation between differents into one between similars abstractly thought of as more real.[1]

The overthrow of perception by conception took a long time to complete itself in this field. Occasionalism The first step was the theory of 'occasionalism,' to which Descartes led the way by his doctrine that mental and physical substance, the one consisting purely of thought, the other purely of extension, were absolutely dissimilar. If this were so, any such causal intercourse as we instinctively perceive between mind and body ceased to be rational.

---

[1] Sir William Hamilton expresses this very compactly: 'What is the law of Causality? Simply this, — that when an object is presented phenomenally as commencing, we cannot but suppose that the complement (i. e. the amount) of existence, which it now contains, has previously been; — in other words, that all that we at present know as an effect must previously have existed in its causes; though what these causes are we may perhaps be altogether unable to surmise.' (End of Lecture 39 of the *Metaphysics*.) The cause becomes a reason, the effect a consequence; and since logical consequence follows only from the same to the same, the older vaguer causation-philosophy develops into the sharp rationalistic dogma that cause and effect are two names for one persistent being, and that if the successive moments of the universe be causally connected, no genuine novelty leaks in.

For thinkers of that age, 'God' was the great solvent of absurdities. He could get over every contradiction. Consequently Descartes' disciples Régis and Cordemoy, and especially Geulincx, denied the fact of psychological interaction altogether. God, according to them, immediately caused the changes in our mind of which events in our body, and those in our body of which events in our mind, appear to be the causes, but of which they are in reality only the signals or occasions.

Leibnitz took the next step forward in quenching the claim to truth of our percep-
Leibnitz   tions. He freed God from the duty of lending all this hourly assistance, by supposing Him to have decreed on the day of creation that the changes in our several minds should coincide with those in our several bodies, after the manner in which clocks, wound up on the same day, thereafter keep time with one another. With this 'pre-established harmony' so-called, the conceptual translation of the immediate given, with its never failing result of negating both activity and continuity, is

complete. Instead of the dramatic flux of personal life, a bare 'one to one correspondence' between the terms of two causally unconnected series is set up. God is the sole cause of anything, and the cause of everything at once. The theory is as monistic as the rationalist heart can desire, and of course novelty would be impossible if it were true.

David Hume made the next step in discrediting common-sense causation. In the chapters on 'the idea of necessary connection' both in his 'Treatise on Human Nature,' and in his 'Essays,' he sought for a positive picture of the 'efficacy of the power' which causes are **Hume** assumed to exert, and failed to find it. He shows that neither in the physical nor in the mental world can we abstract or isolate the 'energy' transmitted from causes to effects. This is as true of perception as it is of imagination. 'All ideas are derived from and represent impressions. We never have any impression that contains any power or efficacy. We never therefore have any idea of power.' 'We never can by our utmost scrutiny discover anything

196

but one event following another; without being able to comprehend any force or power, by which the cause operates, or any connection between it and its supposed effect. . . . The necessary conclusion seems to be that we have no idea of connection or power at all, and that these words are absolutely without any meaning, when employed either in philosophical reasonings or in common life.' 'Nothing is more evident than that the mind cannot form such an idea of two objects as to conceive any connection between them, or comprehend distinctly that power or efficacy by which they are united.'

The pseudo-idea of a connection which we have, Hume then goes on to show, is nothing but the misinterpretation of a mental custom. When we have often experienced the same sequence of events, 'we are carried by habit, upon the appearance of the first one, to expect its usual attendant, and to believe that it will exist. . . . This customary transition of the imagination is the sentiment or impression from which we form the idea of power or neces-

sary connection. Nothing farther is in the case.'
'A cause is an object precedent and contiguous
to another, and so united with it that the idea
of the one determines the idea of the other.'

Nothing could be more essentially pluralistic than the elements of Hume's philosophy.
He makes events rattle against their neighbors
as drily as if they were dice in a box. He might
with perfect consistency have believed in real
novelties, and upheld freewill. But I said
awhile ago that most empiricists had been half-
hearted; and Hume was perhaps the most
half-hearted of the lot. In his essay 'on liberty
and necessity,' he insists that the sequences
which we experience, though between events
absolutely disconnected, are yet absolutely
uniform, and that nothing genuinely new can
flower out of our lives.

The reader will recognize in Hume's famous
pages a fresh example of the way in which conceptual translations always maltreat
fact. Perceptually or concretely (as
we shall notice in more detail later)causation
names the manner in which some fields of con-

Criticism
of Hume

sciousness introduce other fields. It is but one of the forms in which experience appears as a continuous flow. Our names show how successfully we can discriminate within the flow. But the conceptualist rule is to suppose that where there is a separate name there ought to be a fact as separate; and Hume, following this rule, and finding no such fact corresponding to the word 'power,' concludes that the word is meaningless. By this rule every conjunction and preposition in human speech is meaningless — *in, on, of, with, but, and, if,* are as meaningless as *for,* and *because.* The truth is that neither the elements of fact nor the meanings of our words are separable as the words are. The original form in which fact comes is the perceptual *durcheinander,* holding terms as well as relations in solution, or interfused and cemented. Our reflective mind abstracts divers aspects in the muchness, as a man by looking through a tube may limit his attention to one part after another of a landscape. But abstraction is not insulation; and it no more breaks reality than the tube breaks the landscape.

Concepts are notes, views taken on reality,[1] not pieces of it, as bricks are of a house. Causal activity, in short, may play its part in growing fact, even though no substantive 'impression' of it should stand out by itself. Hume's assumption that any factor of reality must be separable, leads to his preposterous view, that no relation can be real. 'All events,' he writes, 'seem entirely loose and separate. One event follows another, but we never can observe any tie between them. They seem conjoined, but never connected.' Nothing, in short, belongs with anything else. Thus does the intellectualist method pulverize perception and triumph over life. Kant and his successors all espoused Hume's opinion that the immediately given is a disconnected 'manifold.' But unwilling simply to accept the manifold, as Hume did, they invoked a superior agent in the shape of what Kant called the 'transcendental ego of apperception' to patch its bits together by synthetic 'categories.' Among these categories Kant inscribes that of 'causality,' and in many quar-

[1] These expressions are Bergson's.

ters he passes for a repairer of the havoc that Hume made.

His chapter on Cause[1] is the most confusedly written part of his famous Critique, and its meaning is often hard to catch. As I understand his text, he leaves things just where Hume did, save that where Hume says 'habit' **Kant** he says 'rule.' They both cancel the notion that phenomena called causal ever exert 'power,' or that a single case would ever have suggested cause and effect. In other words Kant contradicts common sense as much as Hume does and, like Hume, translates causation into mere time-succession; only, whereas the order in time was essentially 'loose' for Hume and only subjectively uniform, Kant calls its uniformity 'objective as obtaining in conformity to a law, which our *Sinnlichkeit* receives from our *Verstand*.' Non-causal sequences can be reversed; causal ones follow in conformity to rule.[2]

[1] Entitled 'The Second Analogy of Experience,' it begins on page 232 of the second edition of his *Critique of Pure Reason*.

[2] Kant's whole notion of a 'rule' is inconstruable by me. What or whom does the rule bind? If it binds the phenomenon that follows

The word *Verstand* in Kant's account must not be taken as if the rule it is supposed to set to sensation made us understand things any better. It is a brute rule of sequence which reveals no 'tie.' The non-rationality of such a 'category' leaves it worthless for purposes of insight. It removes dynamic causation and substitutes no other explanation for the sequences found. It yields external descriptions only, and assimilates all cases to those where we discover no reason for the law ascertained.

Our 'laws of nature' do indeed in large part enumerate bare coexistences and successions. Yellowness and malleability coexist in gold; redness succeeds on boiling in lobsters; coagu-

(the 'effect') we fall back into the popular dynamic view, and any single case would exhibit causal action, even were there no other cases in the world. — Or does it bind the observer of the single case? But his own sensations of sequence are what bind him. Be a sequence causal or non-causal, if it is sensible, he cannot turn it backwards as he can his ideas. Or does the rule bind future sequences and determine them to follow in the same order which the first sequence observed? Since it obviously does not do this when the observer judges wrongly that the first sequence is causal, all we can say is that it is a rule whereby his expectations of uniformity follow his causal judgments, be these latter true or false. But wherein would this differ from the humean position? Kant, in short, flounders, and in no truthful sense can one keep repeating that he has 'refuted Hume.'

lation in eggs; and to him who asks for the Why of these uniformities, science only replies: Positivism 'Not yet'! Meanwhile the laws are potent for prediction, and many writers on science tell us that this is all we can demand. To explain, according to the way of thinking called positivistic, is only to substitute wider or more familiar, for narrower or less familiar laws, and the laws at their widest only express uniformities empirically found. Why does the pump suck up water? Because the air keeps pressing it into the tube. Why does the air press in? Because the earth attracts it. Why does the earth attract it? Because it attracts everything — such attraction being in the end only a more universal sort of fact. Laws, according to their view, only generalize facts, they do not connect them in any intimate sense.[1]

Against this purely inductive way of treating causal sequences, a more deductive inter-

[1] For expressions of this view the student may consult J. S. Mill's *Logic*, book 3, chap. xii; W. S. Jevons's *Principles of Science*, book 6; J. Venn's *Empirical Logic*, chap. xxi, and K. Pearson's *Grammar of Science*, chap. iii.

pretation has recently been urged. If the later member of a succession could be deduced Deductive theories of causation by logic from the earlier member, in the particular sequence the 'tie' would be unmistakable. But logical ties carry us only from sames to sames; so this last phase of scientific method is at bottom only the scholastic principle of *Causa æquat effectum*, brought into sharper focus and illustrated more concretely. It is thoroughly monistic in its aims, and if it could be worked out in detail it would turn the real world into the procession of an eternal identity, with the appearances, of which we are perceptually conscious, occurring as a sort of by-product to which no 'scientific' importance should be attached.[1] In any case no real growth and no real novelty could effect an entrance into life.[2]

[1] 'Consciousness,' writes M. Couturat, to cite a handy expression of this mode of thought, 'is properly speaking, the realm of the unreal. . . . What remains in our subjective consciousness, after all objective facts have been projected and located in space and time, is the rubbish and residuum of the construction of the universe, the formless mass of images that were unable to enter into the system of nature and put on the garment of reality ' *(Revue de Métaphysique*, etc., v, 244).

[2] I avoid amplifying this conception of cause and effect. An immense number of causal facts can indeed be explained satisfactorily by as-

NOVELTY AND CAUSATION

This negation of real novelty seems to be the upshot of the conceptualist philosophy of causation. This is why I called it on page 189 Summary and conclusion the classic obstacle to the acceptance of pluralism's additive world. The principle of causality begins as a hybrid between common sense and intellectualism: — what actively produces an effect, it says, must 'in some way' contain the 'power' of it already.

suming that the effect is only a later position of the cause; and for the remainder we can fall back on the *aliquo modo* which gave such comfort in the past. Such an interpretation of nature would, of course, relegate variety, activity, and novelty to the limbo of illusions, as fast as it succeeded in making its static concepts cancel living facts. It is hard to be sincere, however, in following the conceptual method ruthlessly; and of the writers who think that in science causality must mean identity, some willingly allow that all such scientific explanation is more or less artificial, that identical 'molecules' and 'atoms' are like identical 'pounds' and 'yards,' only pegs in a conceptual arrangement for hanging percepts on in 'one to one relations,' so as to predict facts in 'elegant' or expeditious ways. This is the view of the conceptual universe which our own discussion has insisted on; and, taking scientific logic in this way, no harm is done. Almost no one is radical in using scientific logic metaphysically. Readers wishing for more discussion of the monistic view of cause, may consult G. H. Lewes: *Problems of Life and Mind*, problem 5, chap. iii; A. Riehl: *Der philosophische Kriticismus* (1879), 2ter Absn., Kap **2** ; G. Heymans: *Die Gesetze u. Elemente d. wissenschaftlichen Denkens*, par. 83–85. Compare also B. P. Bowne: *Metaphysics*, revised edition, part i, chap. iv. Perhaps the most instructive general discussion of causation is that in C. Sigwart: *Logic*, 2d edition, par. 73. Chap. v of book 3 in J. S. Mill's *Logic* may be called classical.

But as nothing corresponding to the concept of power can be insulated, the activity-feature of the sequence erelong gets suppressed, and the vague latency, supposed to exist *aliquo modo* in the causal phenomenon, of the effect about to be produced, is developed into a static relation of identity between two concepts which the mind substitutes for the percepts between which the causal tie originally was found.[1]

The resultant state of 'enlightened opinion' about cause, is, as I have called it before, confused and unsatisfactory. Few philosophers hold radically to the identity view. The view of the logicians of science is easier to believe

[1] I omit saying anything in my text about 'energetics.' Popular writers often appear to think that 'science' has demonstrated a monistic principle called 'energy,' which they connect with activity on the one hand and with quantity on the other. So far as I understand this difficult subject, 'energy' is not a principle at all, still less an active one. It is only a collective name for certain amounts of immediate perceptual reality, when such reality is measured in definite ways that allow its changes to be written so as to get constant sums. It is not an ontological theory at all, but a magnificent economic schematic device for keeping account of the functional variations of the surface phenomena. It is evidently a case of '*non fingo* hypotheses,' and since it tolerates perceptual reality, it ought to be regarded as neutral in our causal debate.

but not easier to believe metaphysically, for it violates instinct almost as strongly. Mathematicians make use, to connect the various interdependencies of quantities, of the general concept of function. That A is a function of B (A equals B) means that with every alteration in the value of A, an alteration in that of B is always connected. If we generalize so as also to include qualitative dependencies, we can conceive the universe as consisting of nothing but elements with functional relations between them; and science has then for its sole task the listing of the elements and the describing in the simplest possible terms the functional 're-lations.'[1] Changes, in short, occur, and ring throughout phenomena, but neither reasons, nor activities in the sense of agencies, have any place in this world of scientific logic, which compared with the world of common sense, is so abstract as to be quite spectral, and merits the appellation (so often quoted from Mr. Bradley) of 'an unearthly ballet of bloodless categories.'

[1] W. Jerusalem: *Einleitung in die Philosophie*, 4te Aufl., 145.

CHAPTER XIII

NOVELTY AND CAUSATION — THE PERCEPTUAL VIEW

Most persons remain quite incredulous when they are told that the rational principle of causality has exploded our native belief in naïf activity as something real, and our assumption that genuinely new fact can be created by work done. 'Le sens de la vie qui s'indigne de tant de discours,' awakens in them and snaps its fingers at the 'critical' view. The present writer has also just called the critical view an incomplete abstraction. But its 'functional laws' and schematisms are splendidly useful, and its negations are true oftener than is commonly supposed. We feel as if our 'will' immediately moved our members, and we ignore the brain-cells whose activity that will must first arouse; we think we cause the bell-ring, but we only close a contact and the battery in the cellar rings the bell; we think a certain star's light is the cause of our now seeing it, but ether-waves are the causes, and the star

208

may have been extinguished long ago. We call the 'draft,' the cause of our 'cold'; but without co-operant microbes the draft could do no harm.

Defects of the perceptual view do not warrant scepticism Mill says that causes must be unconditional antecedents, and Venn that they must be 'close' ones. In nature's numerous successions so many links are hidden, that we seldom know exactly which antecedent is unconditional or which is close. Often the cause which we name only fits some other cause for producing the phenomenon; and things, as Mill says, are frequently then most active when we assume them to be acted upon.

This vast amount of error in our instinctive perceptions of causal activity encourages the conceptualist view. A step farther, and we suspect that to suppose causal activity anywhere may be a blunder, and that only consecutions and juxtapositions can be real. Such sweeping scepticism is, however, quite uncalled for. Other parts of experience expose us to error, yet we do not say that in them is no truth. We see trains moving at stations, when they are really standing still, or falsely we feel ourselves to be moving, when we are giddy, without such errors leading us to deny that motion anywhere exists. It exists elsewhere; and the problem is to place it rightly. It is the same with all other illusions of sense.

There is doubtless somewhere an original perceptual experience of the kind of thing we mean by causation, and that kind of thing we locate in various other places, rightly or wrongly as the case may be. Where now is the typical experience originally got?

Evidently it is got in our own personal activity-situations. In all of these what we feel is that a previous field of 'consciousness' containing (in the midst of its complexity) the

The perceptual experience of causation idea of a result, develops gradually into another field in which that result either appears as accomplished, or else is prevented by obstacles against which we still feel ourselves to press. As I now write, I am in one of these activity situations. I 'strive' after words, which I only half prefigure, but which, when they shall have come, must satisfactorily complete the nascent sense I have of what they ought to be. The words are to run out of my pen, which I find that my hand actuates so obediently to desire that I am hardly conscious either of resistance or of effort. Some of the words come wrong, and then I do feel a resistance, not muscular but mental, which instigates a new instalment of my activity, accompanied by more or less feeling of exertion. If the resistance were to my muscles, the exertion would contain an element of strain or squeeze which is less present where the resistance is only mental. If it proves considerable in either kind I may leave off trying to overcome it; or, on the other hand, I may sustain my effort till I have succeeded in my aim.

It seems to me that in such a continuously developing experiential series our concrete perception of causality is found in operation. If the word have any meaning at all it must mean what there we live through. What 'efficacy' and 'activity' are *known-as* is what these appear.

The experiencer of such a situation feels the push, the obstacle, the will, the strain, the triumph, or the passive giving up, just as he feels the time, the space, the swiftness of intensity, the movement, the weight and color, the pain and pleasure, the complexity, or whatever remaining characters the situation may involve. He goes through all that can ever be imagined where activity is supposed. The word 'activity' has no content save these experiences of process, obstruction, striving, strain, or release, ultimate *qualia* as they are of the life given us to be known. No matter what

In it 'final' and 'efficient' causation coincide

'efficacies' there may really be in this extraordinary universe it is impossible to conceive of any one of them being either lived through or authentically known otherwise than in this dramatic shape of something sustaining a felt purpose against felt obstacles, and overcoming or being overcome. What 'sustaining' means here is clear to anyone who has lived through the experience, but to no one else; just as 'loud,' 'red,' 'sweet,' mean something only to beings with ears, eyes, and tongues. The *per-cipi* in these originals of experience is the *esse;* the curtain is the picture. If there is anything hiding in the background, it ought not to be called causal agency, but should get itself an-other name.

The way in which we feel that our successive fields continue each other in these cases is evi-dently what the orthodox doctrine means when it vaguely says that 'in some way' the cause 'contains' the effect. It contains it by propos-ing it as the end pursued. Since the desire of that end is the efficient cause, we see that in the total fact of personal activity final and efficient causes coalesce. Yet the effect is often-est contained *aliquo modo* only, and seldom explicitly foreseen. The activity sets up more effects than it proposes literally. The end is defined beforehand in most cases only as a
And novel-ties arise
general direction, along which all sorts of novelties and surprises lie in wait. These words I write even now surprise me; yet I adopt them as effects of my scripto-rial causality. Their being 'contained' means

213

only their harmony and continuity with my general aim. They 'fill the bill' and I accept them, but the exact shape of them seems determined by something outside of my explicit will.

If we look at the general mass of things in the midst of which the life of men is passed, and ask 'How came they here?' the only broad answer is that man's desires preceded and produced them. If not all-sufficient causes, desire and will were at any rate what John Mill calls unconditional causes, indispensable causes namely, without which the effects could not have come at all. Human causal activity is the only known unconditional antecedent of the works of civilization; so we find, as Edward Carpenter says,[1] something like a law of nature, the law that a movement from feeling to thought and thence to action, from the world of dreams to the world of things, is everywhere going on. Since at each phase of this movement novelties turn up, we may fairly ask, with Carpenter, whether we are not here witnessing in our own personal experience what is really

[1] *The Art of Creation*, 1894, chap. i.

the essential process of creation. Is not the
world really growing in these activities of ours?
And where we predicate activities elsewhere,
have we a right to suppose aught different in
kind from this?

To some such vague vision are we brought
by taking our perceptual experience of action
at its face-value, and following the analogies
which it suggests.

I say vague vision, for even if our desires be
an unconditional causal factor in the only part

Perceptual
causation
sets a
problem

of the universe where we are intimately acquainted with the way
creative work is done, desire is anything but a close factor, even there. The part
of the world to which our desires lie closest is,
by the consent of physiologists, the cortex of
the brain. If they act causally, their first effect
is there, and only through innumerable neural,
muscular, and instrumental intermediaries is
that last effect which they consciously aimed
at brought to birth. Our trust in the face-value
of perception was apparently misleading.
There is no such continuity between cause-and-

215

effect as in our activity-experiences was made to appear. There is disruption rather; and what we naïvely assume to be continuous is separated by causal successions of which perception is wholly unaware.

The logical conclusion would seem to be that even if the kind of thing that causation is, were revealed to us in our own activity, we should be mistaken on the very threshold if we supposed that the fact of it is there. In other words we seem in this line of experience to start with an illusion of place. It is as if a baby were born at a kinetoscope-show and his first experiences were of the illusions of movement that reigned in the place. The nature of movement would indeed be revealed to him, but the real facts of movement he would have to seek outside. Even so our will-acts may reveal the nature of causation, but just where the facts of causation are located may be a further problem.[1] With this further problem, philosophy

[1] With this cause-and-effect are in what is called a transitive relation: as 'more than more is more than less,' so 'cause of cause is cause of effect.' In a chain of causes, intermediaries can drop out and (logically at least) the relation still hold between the extreme terms, the

leaves off comparing conceptual with perceptual experience, and begins enquiring into physical and psychological facts.

Perception has given us a positive idea of causal agency but it remains to be ascertained

This is the problem of the relation of mind to brain
whether what first appears as such, is really such; whether aught else is really such; or finally, whether nothing really such exists. Since with this we are led immediately into the mind-brain relation, and since that is such a complicated topic, we had better interrupt our study of causation provisionally at the present point, meaning to complete it when the problem of the mind's relation to the body comes up for review.

Our outcome so far seems therefore to be only this, that the attempt to treat 'cause,'

Conclusion for conceptual purposes, as a separable link, has failed historically, and has led to the denial of efficient causation, and to the

wider causal span enveloping, without altering the 'closer' one. This consideration may provisionally mitigate the impression of falsehood which psychophysical criticism finds in our consciousness of activity. The subject will come up later in more detail.

substitution for it of the bare descriptive notion of uniform sequence among events. Thus
intellectualist philosophy once more has had
to butcher our perceptual life in order to make
it 'comprehensible.' Meanwhile the concrete
perceptual flux, taken just as it comes, offers
in our own activity-situations perfectly comprehensible instances of causal agency. The
transitive causation in them does not, it is
true, stick out as a separate piece of fact for
conception to fix upon. Rather does a whole
subsequent field grow continuously out of a
whole antecedent field because it seems to yield
new being of the nature called for, while the
feeling of causality-at-work flavors the entire
concrete sequence as salt flavors the water in
which it is dissolved.

If we took these experiences as the type of
what actual causation is, we should have to as-
cribe to cases of causation outside of our own
life, to physical cases also, an inwardly experiential nature. In other words we should have to
espouse a so-called 'pan-psychic' philosophy.
This complication, and the fact that hidden

NOVELTY AND CAUSATION

brain-events appear to be 'closer' effects than those which consciousness directly aims at, lead us to interrupt the subject here provisionally. Our main result, up to this point, has been the contrast between the perceptual and the intellectualist treatment of it.[1]

[1] Almost no philosopher has admitted that perception can give us relations immediately. Relations have invariably been called the work of ' thought,' so cause must be a 'category.' The result is well shown in such a treatment of the subject as Mr. Shadworth Hodgson's, in his elaborate work the *Metaphysic of Experience.* 'What we call conscious activity is not a consciousness of activity in the sense of an immediate perception of it. Try to perceive activity or effort immediately, and you will fail; you will find nothing there to perceive ' (i, 180). As there is nothing there to conceive either, in the discrete manner which Mr. Hodgson desiderates, he has to conclude that 'Causality *per se* (why need it be *per se?*) has no scientific or philosophic justification. . . . All cases of common-sense causality resolve themselves, on analysis, into cases of *post hoc, cum illo, evenit istud.* Hence we say that the search for causes is given up in science and philosophy, and replaced by the search for real conditions (i. e., phenomenal antecedents merely) and the laws of real conditioning.' It must also be recognized that realities answering to the terms cause and causality *per se* are impossible and non-existent' (ii, 374–378).

The author whose discussion most resembles my own (apart from Bergson's, of which more later) is Prof. James Ward in his *Naturalism and Agnosticism* (see the words 'activity' and 'causality' in the index). Consult also the chapter on 'Mental Activity' in G. F. Stout's *Analytic Psychology*, vol. i. W. James's *Pluralistic Universe*, Appendix B, may also be consulted. Some authors seem to think that we do have an ideal conception of genuine activity which none of our experiences, least of all personal ones, match. Hence, and not because activity is a spurious idea altogether, are all the activities we imagine false. Mr. F. H. Bradley seems to occupy some such position, but I am not sure.

APPENDIX

FAITH AND THE RIGHT TO BELIEVE[1]

'INTELLECTUALISM' is the belief that our mind comes upon a world complete in itself, and has the duty of ascertaining its contents; but has no power of re-determining its character, for that is already given.

Among intellectualists two parties may be distinguished. Rationalizing intellectualists lay stress on deductive and 'dialectic' arguments, making large use of abstract concepts and pure logic (Hegel, Bradley, Taylor, Royce). Empiricist intellectualists are more 'scientific,' and think that the character of the world must be sought in our sensible experiences, and found in hypotheses based exclusively thereon (Clifford, Pearson).

Both sides insist that in our conclusions personal preferences should play no part, and that no argument from what *ought to be* to what *is*, is valid. 'Faith,' being the greeting of our whole nature to a kind of world conceived as well adapted to that nature, is forbidden, until purely intellectual *evi-*

---

[1] [The following pages, part of a syllabus printed for the use of students in an introductory course in philosophy, were found with the MS. of this book, with the words, 'To be printed as part of the Introduction to Philosophy,' noted thereon in the author's handwriting. ED.]

dence that such *is* the actual world has come in. Even if evidence should eventually prove a faith true, the truth, says Clifford, would have been 'stolen,' if assumed and acted on too soon.

Refusal to believe anything concerning which 'evidence' has not yet come in, would thus be the rule of intellectualism. Obviously it postulates certain conditions, which for aught we can see need not necessarily apply to all the dealings of our minds with the Universe to which they belong.

1. It postulates that *to escape error* is our paramount duty. Faith *may* grasp truth; but also it *may* not. By resisting it always, we are sure of escaping error; and if by the same act we renounce our chance at truth, that loss is the lesser evil, and should be incurred.

2. It postulates that in every respect the universe is finished in advance of our dealings with it;

That the knowledge of what it thus is, is best gained by a passively receptive mind, with no native sense of probability, or good-will towards any special result;

That 'evidence' not only needs no good-will for its reception; but is able, if patiently waited for, to neutralize ill-will;

Finally, that our beliefs and our acts based thereupon, although they are parts of the world, and although the world without them is unfinished, are yet such mere externalities as not to alter in any way the significance of the rest of the world when they are added to it.

In our dealings with many details of fact these postulates work well. Such details exist in advance of our opinion; truth concerning them is often of no pressing importance; and by believing nothing, we escape error while we wait. But even here we often *cannot* wait but must act, somehow; so we act on the most *probable* hypothesis, trusting that the event may prove us wise. Moreover, not to act on one belief, is often equivalent to acting as if the opposite belief were true, so inaction would not always be as 'passive' as the intellectualists assume. It is one attitude of will.

Again, Philosophy and Religion have to interpret the total character of the world, and it is by no means clear that here the intellectualist postulates obtain. It may be true all the while (even though the evidence be still imperfect) that, as Paulsen says, 'the natural order is at bottom a moral order.' It may be true that work is still doing in the world-process, and that in that work we are called to bear our share. The character of the world's results may in part depend upon our acts. Our acts may depend on our religion, — on our not-resisting our faith-tendencies, or on our sustaining them in spite of 'evidence' being incomplete. These faith-tendencies in turn are but expressions of our good-will towards certain forms of result.

Such faith-tendencies are extremely active psychological forces, constantly outstripping evidence. The following steps may be called the 'faith-ladder':

1. There is nothing absurd in a certain view of the world being true, nothing self-contradictory;

2. It *might* have been true under certain conditions;

3. It *may* be true, even now;

4. It is *fit* to be true;

5. It *ought* to be true;

6. It *must* be true;

7. It *shall* be true, at any rate true for *me*.

Obviously this is no intellectual chain of inferences, like the *sorites* of the logic-books. Yet it is a slope of good-will on which in the larger questions of life men habitually live.

Intellectualism's proclamation that our good-will, our 'will to believe,' is a pure disturber of truth, is itself an act of faith of the most arbitrary kind. It implies the will to insist on a universe of intellectualist constitution, and the willingness to stand in the way of a pluralistic universe's success, such success requiring the good-will and active faith, theoretical as well as practical, of all concerned, to make it 'come true.'

Intellectualism thus contradicts itself. It is a sufficient objection to it, that if a 'pluralistically' organized, or 'co-operative' universe or the 'melioristic' universe above, were really here, the veto of intellectualism on letting our good-will ever have any vote would debar us from ever admitting that universe to be true.

Faith thus remains as one of the inalienable birth-rights of our mind. Of course it must remain a practical, and not a dogmatic attitude. It must go with toleration of other faiths, with the search for the most probable, and with the full consciousness of responsibilities and risks.

It may be regarded as a formative factor in the universe, if we be integral parts thereof, and co-determinants, by our behavior, of what its total character may be.

How we Act on Probabilities

In most emergencies we have to act on probability, and incur the risk of error.

'Probability' and 'possibility' are terms applied to things of the conditions of whose coming we are (to some degree at least) ignorant.

If we are entirely ignorant of the conditions that

make a thing come, we call it a 'bare' possibility. If we know that some of the conditions already exist, it is for us in so far forth a 'grounded' possibility. It is in that case *probable* just in proportion as the said conditions are numerous, and few hindering conditions are in sight.

When the conditions are so numerous and confused that we can hardly follow them, we treat a thing as probable in proportion to the *frequency* with which things of that *kind* occur. Such frequency being a fraction, the probability is expressed by a fraction. Thus, if one death in 10,000 is by suicide, the antecedent probability of my death being a suicide is 1-10,000th. If one house in 5000 burns down annually, the probability that my house will burn is 1-5000th, etc.

Statistics show that in most kinds of thing the frequency is pretty regular. Insurance companies bank on this regularity, undertaking to pay (say) 5000 dollars to each man whose house burns, provided he and the other house-owners each pay enough to give the company that sum, plus something more for profits and expenses.

The company, hedging on the large number of cases it deals with, and working by the long run, need run no risk of loss by the single fires.

The individual householder deals with his own

APPENDIX

single case exclusively. The probability of his house burning is only 1-5000, but if that lot befall he will lose everything. He has no 'long run' to go by, if his house takes fire, and he can't hedge as the company does, by taxing his more fortunate neigh-bors. But in this particular kind of risk, the company helps him out. It translates his one chance in 5000 of a big loss, into a certain loss 5000 times smaller, and the bargain is a fair one on both sides. It is clearly better for the man to lose *certainly*, but *fractionally*, than to trust to his 4999 chances of no loss, and then have the improbable chance befall.

But for most of our emergencies there is no insur-ance company at hand, and fractional solutions are impossible. Seldom can we *act* fractionally. If the probability that a friend is waiting for you in Bos-tion is 1-2, how should you act on that probability? By going as far as the bridge? Better stay at home! Or if the probability is 1-2 that your partner is a villain, how should you act on that probability? By treating him as a villain one day, and confiding your money and your secrets to him the next? That would be the worst of all solutions. In all such cases we must act wholly for one *or* the other horn of the dilemma. We must go in for the more probable alternative as if the other one did not exist, and suffer the full penalty if the event belie our faith.

Now the metaphysical and religious alternatives are largely of this kind. We have but this one life in which to take up our attitude towards them, no insurance company is there to cover us, and if we are wrong, our error, even though it be not as great as the old hell-fire theology pretended, may yet be momentous. In such questions as that of the *character* of the world, of life being moral in its essential meaning, of our playing a vital part therein, etc., it would seem as if a certain *wholeness* in our faith were necessary. To calculate the probabilities and act fractionally, and treat life one day as a farce, and another day as a very serious business, would be to make the worst possible mess of it. Inaction also often counts as action. In many issues the inertia of one member will impede the success of the whole as much as his opposition will. To refuse, *e. g.*, to testify against villainy, is practically to help it to prevail.[1]

The Pluralistic or Melioristic Universe

Finally, if the 'melioristic' universe were *really* here, it would require the active good-will of all of us, in the way of belief as well as of our other activities, to bring it to a prosperous issue.

The melioristic universe is conceived after a

---

[1] Cf. Wm. James: *The Will to Believe*, etc., pp. 1–31, and 90–110.

social analogy, as a pluralism of independent powers. It will succeed just in proportion as more of
these work for its success. If none work, it will fail.
If each does his best, it will not fail. Its destiny
thus hangs on an *if*, or on a lot of *ifs* — which
amounts to saying (in the technical language of
logic) that, the world being as yet unfinished, its
total character can be expressed only by *hypothetical* and not by *categorical* propositions.

(Empiricism, believing in possibilities, is willing
to formulate its universe in hypothetical propositions. Rationalism, believing only in impossibili-
ties and necessities, insists on the contrary on their
being categorical.)

As individual members of a pluralistic universe,
we must recognize that, even though we do *our* best,
the other factors also will have a voice in the result.
If they refuse to conspire, our good-will and labor
may be thrown away. No insurance company can
here cover us or save us from the risks we run in
being part of such a world.

We *must* take one of four attitudes in regard to
the other powers: either

1. Follow intellectualist advice: wait for evidence; and while waiting, do nothing; or

2. *Mistrust* the other powers and, sure that the
universe will fail, *let* it fail; or

APPENDIX

3. *Trust* them; and at any rate do *our* best, in spite of the *if;* or, finally,

4. *Flounder*, spending one day in one attitude, another day in another.

This 4th way is no systematic solution. The 2d way spells faith in failure. The 1st way may in practice be indistinguishable from the 2d way. The 3d way seems the only wise way.

'*If* we do *our* best, *and* the other powers do *their* best, the world will be perfected' — this proposition expresses no actual fact, but only the complexion of a fact thought of as eventually possible. As it stands, *no* conclusion can be positively deduced from it. *A conclusion would require another premise of fact, which only we can supply. The original proposition* per se *has no pragmatic value whatsoever, apart from its power to challenge our will to produce the premise of fact required.* Then indeed the perfected world emerges as a logical conclusion.

We can *create* the conclusion, then. We can and we may, as it were, jump with both feet off the ground into or towards a world of which we trust the other parts to meet our jump — and *only so* can the *making* of a perfected world of the pluralistic pattern ever take place. Only through our precursive trust in it can it come into being.

There is no inconsistency anywhere in this, and

no 'vicious circle' unless a circle of poles holding themselves upright by leaning on one another, or a circle of dancers revolving by holding each other's hands, be 'vicious.'

The faith circle is so congruous with human nature that the only explanation of the veto that intellectualists pass upon it must be sought in the offensive character *to them* of the faiths of certain concrete persons.

Such possibilities of offense have, however, to be put up with on empiricist principles. The long run of experience may weed out the more foolish faiths. Those who held them will then have failed: but without the wiser faiths of the others the world could never be perfected.

(Compare G. Lowes Dickinson: "Religion, a Criticism and a Forecast," N. Y. 1905, Introduction; and chaps. iii, iv.)

INDEX

Absolute idealism, 137; defects of, 138.

Activity, intellectually incomprehensible, 85.

Alembert, d', 114.

Al-Ghazzali, 117 *note.*

Anaxagoras, 11.

Anselm, St., 43 *note.*

Antinomies, Kant's, 160.

Aquinas, St. Thomas, 11, 12, 43.

Archimedes, 148.

Aristotle, 7, 11, 12, 24, 34, 36, 38, 53, 55 *note*, 65, 148, 150 *note*, 190.

Bakewell, C. M., 54 *note*, 116 *note.*

Baldwin, J. M., 6 *note.*

Bax, Belfort, 101 *note.*

Being, problem of, 38; various treatments of problem of, 40; rationalist and empiricist treatments, 42 ; Hegel's mediation of with non-being, 44 ; same amount of must be begged by all, 45; conservation *vs.* creation of, 45.

Bergson, 37, 91, 92, 93, 96, 97 *note*, 200 *note*, 219 *note.*

Berkeley, 37, 121, 122.

Bossuet, 54 *note.*

Bouillier, F., 116 *note.*

Bowne, B. P., 124 *note*, 205 *note.*

Boyle, 20, 21.

Bradley, 84, 91, 92, 93, 94, 107 *note*, 207, 219 *note*, 221.

Burnet, J., 157 *note.*

Cairds, the, 85.

Calderwood, H., 156 *note.*

Cantor, 174, 177, 182.

Carpenter, E., 214.

Cauchy, 184.

Causation, 85; Aristotle on, 190; scholasticism on efficient, 191; occasionalistic theory of, 194; Leibnitz on, 195; Hume on, 196; criticism of Hume on, 198; Kant on, 200; positivism on, 203; deductive theories of, 204; conceptual view of negates novelty, 205; defects of perceptual view of do not warrant scepticism, 209; nature of perceptual experience of, 210; ' final ' and ' efficient ' mingle in perceptual experience, 212; perceptual, sets a problem, 215.

Change, conceptually impossible, 87.

Clerk-Maxwell, 66.

Clifford, 221, 222.

Coleridge, 34.

Comte, A., 16.

Concatenation, unity by, 129.

Conception, a secondary process, 79; and novelty, 154.

Concepts, distinguished from percept, 48; discreteness of, 48; interpenetrate with percepts, 52; dignity of knowledge of, 54; content and function of, 58; originate in utility, 63; theoretic use of, 65; in the *a priori* sciences, 67; in physics, 70; bring new values, 71; rôle of in human life, 73; secondary formations, 79; inadequate, 81; static, 85; Bradley on, 92; self-sameness of, 102;

INDEX

INDEX

INDEX

Russell, B., 174, 179, 180, 181, 183, 186 *note.*
Ruyssen, Th., 50 *note.*

' Same,' meaning of, 103.
Santayana, G., 54 *note.*
Sceptics, pyrrhonian, 91.
Schiller, F. C. S., 37, 109 *note.*
Schopenhauer, 26; on the origin of the problem of being, 38, 50 *note.*
Science, history of, 20; as specialized philosophy, 21; and novelty, 149.
Self-sameness of ideal objects, 102.
Sigwart, C., 205 *note.*
Silberstein, S. J., 120 *note.*
Socrates, 37.
Spencer, Herbert, 13, 27, 33, 42, 65 *note.*
Spinoza, 36, 42, 120 *note*, 121, 136, 137 *note.*
Stallo, J. B., 90 *note.*
Stevenson, 39.
Stewart, Prof. A. J., 55 *note.*
Stöckl, A., 119 *note.*
Stout. G. F., 219 *note.*
Suarez, 12.
Substance, monism of, 119; critique of, 121.

Sympathetic magic, the primitive philosophy, 17.

Taine, H., 59 *note.*
Tannery, Paul, 157 *note.*
Taylor, A. E., 101 *note*, 223.
Thales, 11.
Thomson, J. C., 117 *note.*
Torricelli, 20.
'Transfinite numbers,' 177.

Unity, by concatenation, 129; of purpose, 131; of origin, 132; cash value of, 133; value of, 136

Values, of philosophy, 6; new, brought by concepts, 71.
Voltaire, 20, 26.

Wallace, W., 57 *note*, 75 *note.*
Ward, J., 24 *note*, 219 *note.*
Waterton, S., 184 *note.*
Whewell, W., 19.
Wilbois, 91 *note.*
Wolff, C., 14, 31.

Zeno, 41, 88, 156, 157, 158, 159, 170, 179, 186 *note.*